Walking with Jesus

Other Works by Al Hill

Our Evil—God's Good
And Other Sermons from Genesis through Joshua

Things That Kings Can't Do
And Other Sermons from Judges through 2nd Kings, and the Wisdom Books

In the Presence of the Lord
And Other Sermons from the Psalms and the Prophets

God's Purpose for Your Faith
And Other Sermons from the Gospel of Mark, Hebrews, James and 1st Peter

From Jerusalem to Jericho
And Other Sermons from the Gospel of Luke and the Acts of the Apostles

Traits of the Shepherd
And Other Sermons from the Gospel of John, 1st John and Revelation

Making Peace with Your Father
And Other Sermons from Paul's Letters to the Romans and Corinthians

The Empty God
And Other Sermons from the Shorter Letters of Paul

O Come, Let God Adore Us
And Other Sermons for Advent and Christmas

Not Exactly What They Expected
And Other Sermons for Holy Week and Easter

Dear Trinity
Letters from a Pastor to His People

Walking with Jesus
And Other Sermons from the Gospel of Matthew

Al Hill

SOMMERTON
HOUSE

Copyright © 2018 Al Hill

All rights reserved. No part of this book may be used or reproduced by any means, graphic, electronic, or mechanical, including photocopying, recording, taping or by any information storage retrieval system without the written permission of the author except in the case of brief quotations embedded in critical articles and reviews.

Scripture quotations marked "KJV" are from the King James Version of the Bible.

Scripture quotations marked "RSV" are from the Revised Standard Version of the Bible, copyright © 1946, 1952, and 1971 by the National Council of the Churches of Christ in the United States of America. Used by permission. All rights reserved.

Scripture quotations marked "NASB" are taken from the New American Standard Bible® (NASB), Copyright © 1960, 1962, 1963, 1968, 1971, 1972, 1973,1975, 1977, 1995 by The Lockman Foundation Used by permission. www.Lockman.org

Scripture quotations marked "NIV" are from the Holy Bible, New International Version®, NIV®, copyright © 1973, 1978, 1984, and 2011 by Biblica, Inc.™ Used by permission of Zondervan. All rights reserved worldwide.

Scripture marked "NKJV" is taken from the New King James Version®. Copyright © 1982 by Thomas Nelson. Used by permission. All rights reserved.

Scripture quotations marked "NRSV" are from the New Revised Standard Bible, copyright © 1989 by the National Council of the Churches of Christ in the United States of America. Used by permission. All rights reserved.

Scripture quotations marked "ESV" are from the ESV® Bible (The Holy Bible, English Standard Version®), copyright © 2001 by Crossway, a publishing ministry of Good News Publishers. Used by permission. All rights reserved.

Because of the dynamic nature of the Internet, any web addresses or links contained in this book may have changed since publication and may no longer be valid.

Cover design by the author.
The stock imagery of a stained-glass window depicting Jesus saving Simon Peter when the latter tried to walk on the water to Jesus © istock.

ISBN: 978-1-948773-15-7 (sc)

Library of Congress Control Number: 2018904441

To learn more about or purchase this or other works by Al Hill,
go to www.sommertonhouse.com,
or www.amazon.com/author/alhill.

Dedication

To the memory of my daughter, Meredith,

who inspired a sermon,
and the title of this book,
with something she wrote as a young adult:

"I could never relate to this story before....
I mean: *Who walks on water?!*
But now I look back
and see the moments when I doubted and sank.
Aside from those,
I've been walking on water for years."

Contents

Dedication v
Preface ix

Sermons

Chapter 1. Inauguration Day 5
Chapter 2. Tempted As We Are 13
Chapter 3. The New Guy in Town 23
Chapter 4. God's Wellness Plan 31
Chapter 5. Bizarre Blessings 39
Chapter 6. A Lesson in Prayer 47
Chapter 7. The Problem with Prosperity 55
Chapter 8. Will You Give Them Stones? 61
Chapter 9. Just Ask 69
Chapter 10. Free to Bear Good Fruit 77
Chapter 11. Build Your House 85
Chapter 12. Just Passing Through 95
Chapter 13. Look Who's Invited to Dinner 103
Chapter 14. Divine Assignment 109
Chapter 15. The Games of Childhood 117
Chapter 16. Sowing Seeds—Bearing Fruit 121
Chapter 17. Step Out! 129
Chapter 18. Walking with Jesus 137
Chapter 19. A Question of Identity 143
Chapter 20. Listen to Jesus 149

Chapter 21. If Your Brother Sins 153
Chapter 22. Unity, Liberty, Charity 161
Chapter 23. Vineyard Work and Vineyard Wages 167
Chapter 24. It's Not Fair 173
Chapter 25. Rendering 179
Chapter 26. The Teacher's Take on Taxes 185
Chapter 27. The Greatest Commandment 193
Chapter 28. Big Shots, Beware! 197
Chapter 29. A Lesson in Leadership 203
Chapter 30. Required to Risk 211
Chapter 31. What a Surprise! 219
Chapter 32. All Authority 223

Indices

Sermon Titles in Alphabetical Order 228
Sermon Texts in Biblical Order 230
Related Sermons in Other Volumes 232
Sermon Texts in Lectionary Order 234
Additional Scriptures Referenced 236

Preface

When we talk about "walking with Jesus," we generally mean doing more than "talking the talk" of Christianity. We mean—well—"walking the walk"—behaving like Jesus said (in Gospels like Matthew) His followers should behave.

Some folks talk about "walking with Jesus" and mean a sense of spiritual and emotional closeness to Jesus. By making the business of being a Christian a high priority in your life—and the primary way of identifying yourself—you can gain a feeling of divine peace and protection in the midst of the daily demands of the world around you—a feeling that is not a bad thing to have.

But if the evidence of the Gospels (including that in Matthew) is to be believed, the original experience of walking with Jesus was more like a forced march than a friendly stroll—more stressful than restful—more heart-stopping and eye-popping than the heart-warming wandering about the Holy Land we conjure up in our meditative mind's eye.

Jesus was a Man on a mission—a divine mission. And He didn't have a lot of time to get that mission accomplished. So walking with Jesus meant keeping up with Jesus as He went briskly about His Father's business. It meant being prepared (even when unprepared) to go with Him to places and into situations that would certainly have been avoided otherwise.

But people did go walking with Jesus, more and more at first—and then less and less, when it became clear where He had in mind to go—ultimately. And even those who kept on walking with Him stumbled a good bit along the way. They slipped and tripped and wandered down a dead-end now and then before they found their way back (or *were found* and *led* back) to the path of the Master.

And those who walked with Him up to (and beyond) a hill called Calvary found that they were able to continue walking with Him, just as He had promised. After Jesus ascended into heaven, walking with Him become no less of a challenge, because it was a journey like none they had ever known—or could have imagined without Him. It was, in many ways, like Peter's effort to walk to Jesus on the waters of the Sea of Galilee: It could not have been done without Jesus beside them, walking with them, bearing them up in miraculous ways.

This is what it means to walk with Jesus: to go where He is going, navigating by His example, upheld at every step by His power. And some among us, knowingly or otherwise, have been walking that way for years.

Walking with Jesus is a collection of 32 sermons from the Gospel of Matthew. All the sermons in this book are based, at least in part, on texts from the first Gospel, though not all the sermons I preached from Matthew are in this book.[1] The sequence of the sermons here follows the order of the biblical texts.

The sermons were preached in Navy chapels and civilian churches over a period of many years, as internal references to events of the times will suggest. Though all were written in full, they were written to be heard (in public) rather than read (in private). As you read, I hope you will be able to "hear" something of what congregations were intended to hear.

---

[1] A list of my sermons from Matthew printed in other books is included in one of the indices at the end of this volume.

Your handicap will be the absence of vocal inflection, facial expression, body language, gestures and shared experiences that helped to convey the original meaning of the words spoken. Your advantage will be your ability to read at your own pace, or stop reading at any point to consider a point, to re-read a sentence—or paragraph—when the words alone have left you confused. You can also "put the sermon down" right in the middle to answer the phone or get yourself a sandwich or take care of some task you just remembered. (We discouraged that sort of thing of the folks in church on Sunday mornings.)

The publication of this book and its "colleagues"[2] is an effort at Christian stewardship. Like most preachers, I spent thousands of hours over a number of decades researching and preparing sermons. What came out of that effort may still be of value to others who are even now proclaiming the good news of our faith. I hope you will find something to inspire, inform or perhaps intrigue you, as the work of so many others did me as I worked to put sermons together for the people of God in my care.

I also believe that something here may stimulate any Christian's spiritual growth and understanding of the faith we share. I hope that will be the case for you. And I have tried across the years to remember that a part of the preacher's job is to present the gospel to anyone who is willing to hear it. So don't be afraid to give a copy of this book to anyone willing to accept it—or to share thoughts from it with someone who may be looking into Christianity from the outside.

❧

The full biblical text for each sermon has been provided in the book either before or within the sermon, as a convenience to you.

---

[2] There are 11 volumes of sermons in this series, three from Old Testament passages, four based primarily on the Gospels, two from the letters of Paul, and one each dedicated to sermons about Advent and Christmas, and Holy Week and Easter, respectively. This is the fifth of these volumes to be published.

The different versions of the Bible used in the book reflect the particular preferences of the various congregations I served.

The footnotes you will find throughout are a later addition, for your benefit. When actually quoting scripture, I have included the version used. When I paraphrased (which I seemed to have done a good deal of), or merely alluded to a passage, no version is provided in the footnote. I have also given scriptural citations for ideas or assertions in the sermons that are based on biblical authority.

Several sermons are based on the same passage. This is to be expected when one has followed the Revised Common Lectionary for many (though not all) of the years in the preaching process. I seldom "re-preached" a sermon, but similarities will be discernable in thought and phrasing. I have included multiple sermons on the same text when they existed because I do not know which would be most useful to you.

I have provided indices at the end that should help the Bible student "navigate" the book more comfortably and profitably. I have appreciated such "helps" (when they existed) in the books of sermons I have consulted over the years. I hope they will be of benefit to you.

And I hope and pray that something in these pages will make the time you spend here a blessing to you and will enhance your ability to walk with Jesus.

Sermons

From Matthew 3

1 Samuel 16:11-13a ESV

Over a thousand years before the birth of Jesus, Israel went from being a loose alliance of 12 tribes to a unified nation with a single king. Because they were the chosen people of God, they believed their king should be chosen by God as well. Samuel, the *religious* leader of Israel, anointed a man named Saul as Israel's first king to signify his divine selection, but when Saul displeased God, God sent Samuel to find and anoint a successor. The person Samuel found was a shepherd boy named David. David was anointed by God's servant and baptized with God's Spirit, Who came upon him in power in the process.

¹¹ So [Samuel] asked Jesse, "Are these all the sons you have?"
"There is still the youngest," Jesse answered, "but he is tending the sheep."
Samuel said, "Send for him; we will not sit down until he arrives."
¹² So he sent and had him brought in. He was ruddy, with a fine appearance and handsome features.
Then the LORD *said, "Rise and anoint him; he is the one."*
¹³ So Samuel took the horn of oil and anointed him in the presence of his brothers, and from that day on the Spirit of the LORD *came upon David in power.*

Inauguration Day

Matthew 3:1, 13-17 ESV

Before Jesus began His public ministry, He underwent a public baptism at the hands of John the Baptist, who was already active in Judea. Though John urged people to be baptized as a sign of their repentance of sin, Jesus had no need for such a baptism, and so His was a sign of something else.

¹ In those days, John the Baptist came, preaching in the Desert of Judea…

¹³ Then Jesus came from Galilee to the Jordan to be baptized by John.
¹⁴ But John tried to deter him, saying, "I need to be baptized by you, and do you come to me?"
¹⁵ Jesus replied, "Let it be so now; it is proper for us to do this to fulfill all righteousness."
Then John consented.
¹⁶ As soon as Jesus was baptized, he went up out of the water. At that moment, heaven was opened, and he saw the Spirit of God descending like a dove and lighting on him. ¹⁷ And a voice from heaven said, "This is my Son, whom I love; with him, I am well pleased."

1.

Inauguration Day

1 Samuel 16:11-13; Matthew 3:1, 13-17 ESV

Today is Inauguration Day.[3] The formal festivities of parades and parties will begin tomorrow with a ceremonial swearing in of the person who will preside over the government of this nation for the next four years. But by law, according to the Constitution, the official oath of office must actually be sworn today, at noon.[4]

And so shortly after we conclude our worship, one four-year presidential term of office will end and a new four-year term will begin with a brief, simple and almost unnoticed event.

The event will be witnessed by a relatively small group of people, and when it is concluded, incredible power and authority will have been bestowed upon one man, and that one man will influence the course of history, for good or ill, until he no longer possesses the power and authority delegated to him—until noon, four years from today, when the *next* presidential inauguration will take place.

As important as today's inauguration will be—and as impressive as tomorrow's inaugural celebrations will seem—we

---

[3] This sermon was preached on January 20, 2013.
[4] *U. S. Constitution*, Article XX (The 20th Amendment), Section 1.

Inauguration Day

have heard today about two inaugurations that are far more significant.

Three thousand years ago, Samuel sought out a shepherd boy in an insignificant little village and anointed him to be the future king of Israel. Young David was officially inaugurated for a position whose power and authority would not be provided him unto many years later when the elders of all the tribes of God's people came to him and publicly asked him to be their king.[5] David began a term in office that day that would last for decades and establish a dynasty of descendants who would rule in David's stead—not for four years—but for four hundred years and more.[6]

And in Samuel's inauguration of David was sown the seed of another inauguration—the inauguration of a special descendant of David Who would not be born for a thousand years.[7] The inauguration of this Son of David to come would take place in the waters of the Jordan River at the hands of another well-respected religious leader while a handful (or a hillside-full) of people looked on, without much awareness of what they were witnessing when Jesus of Nazareth led a very uncomfortable John the Baptist off the bank and into the current that would suffice for the ceremony starting a term in office that will never end.

The baptism of Jesus was His inauguration as the Ruler of the world—the divine and eternal King of kings.[8] That brief, simple, almost unnoticed ceremony in the Jordan River began a reign that will last for all time[9] and encompass all Creation.[10] It was the

---

[5] 2 Samuel 5:1-5
[6] 2 Samuel 7:12; 2 Kings 25:6-7, 27-30.
[7] 2 Samuel 7:16.
[8] 1 Timothy 6:15; Revelation 17:14; 19:16.
[9] Revelation 11:15.
[10] Colossians 1:15-16; Revelation 22:5.

inauguration of One to Whom every knee will bow and of Whom every tongue will confess His Lordship.[11]

The baptism of Jesus is a big deal, but like everyone there (with the exception of John the Baptist), we are likely to miss its importance. So let's go back and look again—this time, with the eyes of understanding.

☙❧

John the Baptist is baptizing Jews, those Jews who have heard his condemnation of their sins and his call for their repentance.

But *Jews* don't get "baptized." Baptism is for people who want to *become* Jews, who want to renounce their former lives and identities in favor of a higher moral and spiritual life as one of God's Chosen people. Baptism is for proselytes converting to Judaism.[12]

But John is calling Jews to repentance just like they were foreigners—filthy sinners—cut off from God. Because they are. They preach God's word, but they don't practice it.[13] Nobody does—or can. And some are clear-eyed enough to see that—and honest enough to admit it—and courageous enough to step forward and say, "My heritage will not make me right with God—my culture will not keep me from suffering the judgment I deserve. I cannot keep God's law. Only God can wash away my sins and all I can do is ask Him to do it."[14]

And there they go, down in the water, praying some version of "Good Lord, show me the way!"[15]

And then one day, in the midst of all these people who have at least figured out and admitted their problem, Jesus shows up.

---

[11] Philippians 2:10-11.
[12] W. F. Flemington, "Baptism," *Interpreter's Dictionary of the Bible, Volume 1*, New York, NY: Abingdon Press, 1962, p. 348.
[13] Matthew 23:1-3.
[14] See Matthew 18:13.
[15] From "Down in the River to Pray," a traditional Christian folk hymn of unknown origin, popularized in the movie, *O Brother, Where Art Thou*, 2000.

Inauguration Day

Jesus: descendent of King David, born of the Virgin Mary, only-begotten and sinless Son of God the Father[16]—Jesus shows up at John's outdoor revival meeting and says, "Me, too. It's My turn to be 'put under.'"

And John thinks, "Good Lord, You *are* the Way!" and says as much, though not in so many words.

But Jesus says, "Let's go!" and will not take "No" for an answer.

Jews don't get baptized! But Jesus is a Jew, and He's going to get baptized.

Well, only *sinful* Jews get baptized.

But Jesus isn't sinful—never has been, never will be, until, of course, God made Him Who knew no sin to *be* sin, for us.[17] But God hasn't done that yet when Jesus comes down to the Jordan. And He plans to get baptized anyway.

John is baptizing sinful Jews who are repenting their sins. But Jesus has nothing to repent of, and still, He demands that John baptize Him.

꧁꧂

Do you get the sense that *this* is no ordinary baptism? *This* baptism doesn't mean what all the other baptisms mean, just like His crucifixion will not mean what *any* of the other—or *all* the other—crucifixions mean, when they nail His broken body to a cross.

When Jesus goes down in the Jordan River with John—down under the waters flowing over Him like a new grave covering a corpse—His Body held there by John's iron grip—it is neither an act of remorse nor a cry of confession. It is, for Jesus, a solemn acceptance of the office to which He has been appointed. It is an

---

[16] Matthew 1:1; Luke 1:26-31; John 3:16; Hebrews 4:15.
[17] 2 Corinthians 5:21.

anointing—an inauguration—of Jesus, as He assumes the position of Savior of the world.[18]

The angels announced His coming and the significance of His birth.[19] The Holy Spirit pointed Him out to the pious in the temple when He was but days upon the earth.[20] The teachers of the faith were fascinated by Him when He came back to the temple as a boy, already sensing something of His calling.[21]

But how do You know when the time has come to begin saving the world? Where do You go to get started? How do You begin?

Jesus went to the Jordan to be baptized by John. One day, after 30 years of living the life of an average person in an average place—after 30 years, it turns out, of preparation—30 years of potential and promise—Jesus put down the tools of His trade and left the familiar furnishings of home and village, the familiar faces of family and friends—and began a journey to the Jordan that would begin a journey to Calvary that would begin a journey of millions of men and women to heaven.

Jesus began to save the world—and you and me—by doing what those who wanted to be saved were doing, even though He didn't need to be doing it—even though doing what they were doing meant something totally different when Jesus did it.

But that's what Jesus does; that's how He saved—and is still saving—the world. Jesus enters into our lives,[22] foreign to God and filthy with sin though they be,[23] and shares them with us[24] and transforms them into something wholly and wonderfully different

---

[18] John 4:42; 1 John 4:14.
[19] Matthew 1:20-21; Luke 1:26-31; Luke 2:8-11.
[20] Luke 2:22-38.
[21] Luke 2:42-47.
[22] Revelation 3:20.
[23] Isaiah 53:5-6; Romans 3:10, 23.
[24] Hebrews 2:14-15.

Inauguration Day

in the process[25]—just like He did at the Jordan with John and all the "repenters" waiting their turns to wash away their sins.

Jesus went to the Jordan, but He wasn't doing what the rest of them were doing. And because He wasn't, what He was doing there would mean that what everybody else was doing there would accomplish with God what they wanted to have happen when they went down in the water: *They would be saved.*[26]

Jesus went down in the water—and came up out of the water—and His inaugural festivities really began. The heavens were opened—which means, of course, that the way to God that had been closed was opened. And Jesus saw the Holy Spirit descend on Him, which, of course, is what happened to His ancestor David when he was inaugurated as God's chosen ruler long before—which means that the salvation that had been in preparation for so many centuries was now beginning in the person of Jesus. He had been properly and successfully inaugurated.

And a Voice from heaven said, *"This is my Son, whom I love; with him I am well pleased"*—which means the plan of salvation is working perfectly in the person of Jesus.

All this may be true, but even an all-star like John the Baptist was uncomfortable with a process that flew in the face of what he thought God wanted him to do. And what did Jesus say to John?

"Let it be so for now; it is proper for us to do this to fulfill all righteousness."

Jesus comes and says, "Immerse Me. Whatever your qualms or discomfort, just do it. It's what needs to happen."

---

[25] John 10:10; 2 Corinthians 5:17-19.
[26] Acts 2:21; 16:31; Romans 5:9-10; Titus 3:5.

But now He's talking to you and what He means is, "Immerse Me, not in the Jordan or the nearest river you can find, but in your life, in the ebb and flow of your existence—in the dark ground of your consciousness and the deep places of your heart.

"Inaugurate Me as your Savior just as the Heavenly Father has done, so that all righteousness—all the things that are right and godly—can be fulfilled—in you—by Me."

To "inaugurate" is "to induct into an office with suitable ceremonies;" it is "to bring about the beginning of something."[27] Jesus was baptized to inaugurate His reign over us, a reign that would be exercised first by entering into life with us and, with His life, transforming ours.

When you watch the inauguration of others, will you not inaugurate Jesus as your God-given Savior and immerse your life in Him as He has immersed His life in you?

---

[27] "Inaugurate," *Merriam-Webster Dictionary*.

Tempted As We Are

Matthew 3:16—4:11 RSV

3 ⁱ⁶ *And when Jesus was baptized, he went up immediately from the water, and behold, the heavens were opened and he saw the Spirit of God descending like a dove, and alighting on him;* ¹⁷ *and lo, a voice from heaven, saying, "This is my beloved Son, with whom I am well pleased."*

4 ¹*Then Jesus was led up by the Spirit into the wilderness to be tempted by the devil.* ² *And he fasted forty days and forty nights, and afterward he was hungry.* ³ *And the tempter came and said to him, "If you are the Son of God, command these stones to become loaves of bread."* ⁴ *But he answered, "It is written,*

> *Man shall not live by bread alone,*
> *but by every word that proceeds*
> *from the mouth of God.'"*

⁵ *Then the devil took him to the holy city, and set him on the pinnacle of the temple,* ⁶ *and said to him, "If you are the Son of God, throw yourself down; for it is written,*

> *'He will give his angels charge of you,'*

and

> *'On their hands they will bear you up,*
> *lest you strike your foot against a stone.'"*

⁷ *Jesus said to him, "Again it is written,*

> *'You shall not tempt the Lord your God.'"*

⁸ *Again, the devil took him to a very high mountain, and showed him all the kingdoms of the world and the glory of them;* ⁹ *and he said to him, "All these I will give you, if you will fall down and worship me."* ¹⁰ *Then Jesus said to him, "Begone, Satan! for it is written,*

> *'You shall worship the Lord your God*
> *and him only shall you serve.'"*

¹¹ *Then the devil left him, and behold, angels came and ministered to him.*

2.

Tempted As We Are

Matthew 3:16—4:11 RSV

The sermon today is supposed to tell you something about temptation. I have given a good deal of thought to this business of temptation over the years, and I have even had some personal experience with it myself. In fact, over the course of this very week, as the weather improved, I was tempted on several occasions to devote my attention to things other than the preparation of this sermon. After you have heard it, you may suspect that I yielded to those particular temptations. I hope you won't.

Temptation, of course, is related to sin. But temptation is not sin. They are not the same thing. The writer of Hebrews says that Jesus, *"…has been tempted in every way, just as we are—yet was without sin."*[28]

Except for Jesus, we *"all have sinned and come short of the glory of God."*[29] We are all sinners. But we do not sin all the time. There are times when, by the grace of God, we do not sin. Will we sin again? Probably. But here's the little secret the devil does not want you to know: You do not *have* to sin.

---

[28] Hebrews 4:15, ESV.
[29] Romans 3:23, KJV.

Think about it: at each point when you are tempted to sin, you could choose *not* to sin, which means you don't *have* to sin. There is no point at which you *have* to sin, and so at every point, you could "not sin." Scripture confirms this: *"...God is faithful; he will not let you be tempted beyond what you can bear. But when you are tempted, he will also provide a way out so that you can endure it."*[30]

Temptation is not sin, unless you're seeking it, assisting it, relishing it, readily and willingly submitting to it.

Don't give the devil a "free shot on goal." And don't let the devil "con" you out of the joy of your salvation in Christ by making you feel guilty about the thoughts and feelings he keeps urging on you.

It "ain't" sin until you *decide* to think the thoughts or feel the feelings—or do the deeds yourself. Until then, it's just temptation, and Jesus was tempted just like all of us—and it wasn't sin.

You don't have to feel guilty when you're not. You don't have to be ashamed if you haven't done anything shameful. You can be tempted and not sin.

※

On the other hand, you can sin without being tempted. If your conscience has been sufficiently corroded that you no longer have a sense of the difference between good and evil, or of the moral consequences involved in the choices you make, you can rack up some serious sin without the first pang of guilt or shame.[31] For instance, no one—*no one*—involved in the recent Super Bowl halftime degeneracy[32] has confessed, repented—or even acknowledged—that the event they planned months in advance and paid millions of dollars to produce was—in its entirety—an evil, immoral, godless-fertility-cult-like exhibition, devoid of cultural value, and damaging to the moral character of this nation,

---

[30] 1 Corinthians 10:13, NIV.
[31] See Romans 1:18-32.
[32] This sermon was preached in 2004.

From Matthew 3 and 4

while at the same time, undermining our ability to demonstrate to other societies around the world the benefit of our moral leadership in the community of nations.

No performer—famous or otherwise—no technician, no television executive, no commercial sponsor, no representative of professional football—none of the hundreds or perhaps thousands of people involved in causing that incredible carnal display to happen ever said, "Hey, wait a minute. This isn't right. This isn't good. This is sinful and we shouldn't do this sort of thing at all."

In the days that followed, their "deer-in-the-headlights" incomprehension of the criticism, and the clever, calculated, cynically self-excusing responses designed to minimize the impact of that criticism indicated that the problem was not one person's "wardrobe malfunction," but the entire group's "moral awareness malfunction." No one has said, "I'm guilty. I'm ashamed of myself. I knew it was wrong, but I yielded to temptation and sinned." They weren't tempted; they just sinned—and they did so because that is their chosen, accustomed way of life.

But that's them.

What about us?

For us, even as Christians, temptation and sin are seldom far apart. It's a fair bet that all of us face temptation. Some of you are struggling with great temptation even as I speak. You may be waging a heroic effort against the tempter's attack, and coming here today, you seek the power of God to sustain you in the struggle. God give you strength.

Or you may have experienced defeat, perhaps repeatedly, at the tempter's hand, and you come before God broken and ashamed, dreading the next assault that you no longer even hope you will be able to overcome. The temptation now is just to surrender—without a struggle—to admit defeat at the onset to avoid the pain of trying and failing. To you, I say, "Don't. Don't ever give in."

And don't say, "The devil made me do it!"[33] when you do yield to temptation and sin. The devil cannot make you sin. He wants you to think he can, but he can't. Every sin is your personal free choice. That's why it's sin, which separates you from God. James wrote, *"...each person is tempted when he is lured and enticed by his own desire. Then desire when it has conceived gives birth to sin; and sin when it is full-grown brings forth death."*[34] And that's why Jesus died: to overcome the power of death and the wages of sin.[35]

You have a better chance to fight against your temptations when you understand what's going on—when you recognize the struggle for what it really is. The temptation you face is not about you. It's about the God you serve, the God Who loves you and gave His Son Jesus Christ to redeem you from the sins[36] you have committed as a result of yielding to your temptations. The devil doesn't care about you or about what you do—except as it grieves God or complicates God's redemptive work.

The devil doesn't care whether you are bad or good per se—but he is terribly concerned to neutralize your effectiveness as an instrument in the mighty hand of God. That's the point of your temptations. That's why the devil wants you to sin. And the greater your commitment to God—the more obedient and trusting you are—the more necessary to the devil's purpose it is that you be deceived, enticed, seduced—tempted into spiritual uselessness.

We do not *have* to sin when the devil tempts us; but what if we do? What if we do "lose a battle" with the tempter? *"...if anybody does sin, we have an advocate with the Father—Jesus Christ, the Righteous One. He is the atoning sacrifice for our sins, and not only for ours but also for the sins of the whole world."*[37]

---

[33] The favorite excuse of a fictitious character, "Geraldine," made famous in the 1970s by comedian Flip Wilson.
[34] James 1:14-15, RSV.
[35] Hebrews 2:14; Romans 6:23.
[36] John 3:16.
[37] 1 John 2:1-2, NIV.

From Matthew 3 and 4

And *"if we confess our sins, he is faithful and just and will forgive us our sins and purify us from all unrighteousness."*[38]

Poor old devil, he just can't win for losing: He works so hard to knock us down, and when he does, Jesus just picks us back up and cleans us back up and puts us back where we can do the most good for Him. Jesus is like a one-man holy M.A.S.H. unit healing His people on the front lines of the spiritual warfare battlefield.[39]

But as good as it is to know that Jesus will take care of us when we fall victim to our temptations, still better is it to fight the battle against temptation more effectively. So how do we fight temptation effectively? Let's go back to the scripture for some pointers.

☙❧

Notice that this whole wilderness temptation business actually begins with the baptism of Jesus. Our baptism is a sign of submission to Jesus in repentance, faith, and redemption. If you want to fight your temptations effectively, you need to belong to Jesus, and baptism is the first act of obedience demonstrating you do.

When Jesus came up out of the baptismal waters, He saw the Spirit of God descend upon Him. Jesus recognized the presence of the Holy Spirit in His life and knew that the power of the Holy Spirit was available to Him. That same power is available to every believer. Jesus told His disciples, *"…I will ask the Father, and he will give you another advocate to help you and be with you forever—the Spirit of truth. …he lives with you and will be in you."*[40] You think you're on your own when you're faced with some temptation? Never in life, my friend! The Holy Spirit is in you and ready to do battle with and

---

[38] 1 John 1:9, NIV.
[39] As in the popular movie and long-running TV show, *M.A.S.H.* is a military acronym for "Mobile Army Surgical Hospital."
[40] John 14:16-17, NIV.

for you.[41] Recognize Who you've got on your side: *"...greater is he that is in you than he that is in the world."*[42]

Jesus heard the heavenly Voice telling Him Who He was and what God thought about Him. Jesus took His cues about His identity and His value from God. God told Jesus, *"You are my beloved Son, in whom I am well pleased."* Satan said, *"If you are the Son of God, do this...and this..."*

My, how that particular temptation gets around!

"If you want me to acknowledge you as somebody worthwhile—if you want me to treat you like you're somebody important—then do the things I want you to do." It never ends, of course. You remember how it goes: "If you want me to be impressed with you, then smoke this cigarette. If you want me to think you're cool, then drink this beer. If you want my approval, take these drugs, wear these clothes, get these tattoos, have sex, torment the people below you in the pecking order and suck up to those above you."

How long must we play along with Satan's self-destructive game of "If you..., then do..."? Jesus said to His followers, *"I no longer call you servants.... Instead, I have called you friends...."*[43] When you hear Jesus tell you that—and know that you are worth His life's blood poured out on the Cross—you know you've got nothing to prove, no matter whose voice Satan uses and what challenge he offers. You are who God says you are.

The Bible says Jesus followed the leading of the Holy Spirit—even when the Holy Spirit took Him to places He would not have chosen to go to—and positioned Him to deal with situations that were anything but enjoyable. Jesus followed the Holy Spirit into the wilderness.

Have you felt like you were wandering in the wilderness and wondering why? Remember: the wilderness is the place God takes

---

[41] Mark 13:11; Romans 5:5; 1 John 4:13.
[42] 1 John 4:4, KJV.
[43] John 15:15, NIV.

From Matthew 3 and 4

His people to refine and transform them. It's where God took the children of Israel to learn His law after He delivered them from bondage in Egypt.[44] It's where God took the prophet Elijah after destroying the prophets of Baal on Mount Carmel.[45] And it is where the Holy Spirit leads Jesus after His baptism.

If you're following the Holy Spirit, and it seems like a wilderness, then that's probably where God wants you right now—where you may have to face down the tempter for a while (with the Spirit's help) while God prepares you for whatever He intends for you next.

The Bible says Jesus fasted in preparation for His confrontation with Satan. Stuck out in the wilderness, Jesus still could—and did—focus on His need for spiritual nourishment, ignoring His physical needs and desires for a time. Spiritual warfare requires spiritual preparation, and spiritual preparation requires you to organize your life so that you can give the time and attention necessary to God's work in you.[46] Jesus may have been hungry afterwards, but He was more than a match for the devil.

And the devil certainly came after Him.

꙳

Then how come the devil didn't come out so well in his confrontation with Jesus?

Here's why: Jesus evaluated all the temptations of Satan against the guidelines found in God's Word. Even His seemingly acceptable needs Jesus held up to the light of scripture. The Word of God will show you what is right and what is wrong. It will also show you when something that is usually right may (because of the conditions or context) be wrong.

"But the devil quoted scripture himself as he tempted Jesus."

---

[44] Exodus 19:1-6; Hosea 13:4-5.
[45] 1 Kings 18:19-40.
[46] Proverbs 3:6; 2 Timothy 2:4, 15.

Yes, but Jesus recognized "scriptural ventriloquism" when he heard it.[47] You see, when the devil quotes scripture—when Satan impersonates God (as he delights in doing)—the message may sound "religious," but it will always by twisted, distorted, and manipulated for evil purposes.[48] And you can tell the difference if you're listening to hear what God has to say rather than hoping to hear God say what you want to hear. If you're intent on some "particular" word, you may hear it, but it "ain't" necessarily God, even if the speaker is using God's words.

The Bible makes it very clear that Jesus knew He had authority over Satan and that He wasn't afraid to use it. Jesus sent Satan away like the needless nuisance he is. In dealing with the devil, the proper procedure could be described as "Don't ask; do tell." If you ask the devil to stop tempting you—to leave you alone—the answer will always be, "No." Given the option, the devil will always give you hell.

Do not give him the option. Jesus has delegated to every Christian the authority to tell the devil where to go.[49] So do it. Don't play around with his temptations. Don't let him get a foothold in your life. Don't let him flatter your ego or play havoc with your physical appetites.[50] Don't let him lead you down into bitterness or jealousy,[51] or pump you up with self-righteous indignation or pride.[52] Don't let him soak you in shame or regret or smother you with anxiety or depression.

Dismiss the devil with the authority given you by Jesus Christ: *"Be gone, Satan!"*[53] Now, he won't *stay* gone, so every time he slithers back into your thoughts or feelings, throw him right back out again. Zero tolerance! When you recognize and confront the

---

[47] Matthew 12:34; John 8:44; 1 John 4:1.
[48] 2 Corinthians 11:14.
[49] Luke 9:1; 10:17-19.
[50] Genesis 3:1-6.
[51] Genesis 37:4, 8, 18-20, 23-24, 28.
[52] Luke 18:10-12.
[53] Matthew 4:10-11; James 4:7.

tempter, you will be amazed how truly lame his temptations become. It's only when you let him come in and set up shop under some false identity or other[54] and you start listening attentively to his seductive sales pitch that you feel the growing pressure to buy his demonic bill of goods. Don't do it! They will turn sour in a heartbeat and exact a price from you that is infinitely greater than advertised.[55] Satan, be gone!

The devil said to Jesus, *"Command these stones to become bread."* Jesus would instead command the dead to rise.[56] The devil said to Jesus, "Throw yourself down and angels will catch you." Jesus chose instead to be lifted up, to draw all men to Himself.[57] The devil said to Jesus, *"I will give you all the kingdoms of the world."* But Jesus knew that these kingdoms weren't the devil's to give.[58]

God was not afraid to send His Son to take on the devil. And God is not afraid to send us, His children, with the Holy Spirit's help, to do battle with the tempter today.

Be of good courage.

Trust in the Lord.

And send old Satan packing!

---

[54] Matthew 12:43-45.
[55] Romans 3:23.
[56] John 11:43-44; Luke 7:11-15; 8:49-55.
[57] John 3:14; 12:32.
[58] Psalm 24:1.

The New Guy in Town

Matthew 4:12-23 ESV

¹² Now when he heard that John had been arrested, he withdrew into Galilee. ¹³ And leaving Nazareth he went and lived in Capernaum by the sea, in the territory of Zebulun and Naphtali, ¹⁴ so that what was spoken by the prophet Isaiah might be fulfilled:

> ¹⁵ "The land of Zebulun and the land of Naphtali,
> the way of the sea, beyond the Jordan,
> Galilee of the Gentiles—
> ¹⁶ the people dwelling in darkness
> have seen a great light,
> and for those dwelling in the region and shadow of death,
> on them a light has dawned."

¹⁷ From that time Jesus began to preach, saying, "Repent, for the kingdom of heaven is at hand."

¹⁸ While walking by the Sea of Galilee, he saw two brothers, Simon (who is called Peter) and Andrew his brother, casting a net into the sea, for they were fishermen. ¹⁹ And he said to them, "Follow me, and I will make you fishers of men." ²⁰ Immediately they left their nets and followed him. ²¹ And going on from there he saw two other brothers, James the son of Zebedee and John his brother, in the boat with Zebedee their father, mending their nets, and he called them. ²² Immediately they left the boat and their father and followed him.

²³ And he went throughout all Galilee, teaching in their synagogues and proclaiming the gospel of the kingdom and healing every disease and every affliction among the people.

3.

The New Guy in Town

Matthew 4:12-23 ESV

In case you missed the last few weeks, let me bring you up to speed on the story: a baby was born in Bethlehem, accompanied by some very impressive special effects, and given the name Jesus.[59] The baby was carried up to Jerusalem a few weeks later to be "presented" to God at the temple,[60] then taken back to Bethlehem where some unusual foreigners called Magi eventually found Him.[61]

After that, He was hustled off to Egypt[62] so that a bloodthirsty king named Herod wouldn't find Him and slaughter Him the way he slaughtered all the other little boys in and around Bethlehem.[63] Later, when this Herod died, Jesus was brought back to the Holy Land and raised in a nothing town called Nazareth.[64]

As a grown man, Jesus went to have John the Baptist baptize Him in the Jordan River.[65] After that, He took a detour into the

---

[59] Luke 2:4-14; Matthew 1:25.
[60] Luke 2:22.
[61] Matthew 2:1-2, 7-11.
[62] Matthew 2:13-14.
[63] Matthew 2:16.
[64] Matthew 2:19-23.
[65] Matthew 3:13-17.

The New Guy in Town

desert to face down the devil.[66] The tempter tempted Jesus, but turned out to be no match for God's Messiah.

After sending Satan on his way—at least for a while—Jesus heard that John the Baptist had gotten himself arrested, which led Jesus to head back from the desert to His hometown, where He was almost lynched for presenting Himself to His old neighbors, friends and family as the fulfillment of Messianic prophecies.[67]

And that's where we pick things up today. Jesus is ready to start His ministry—to start saving the world. But that's not all He has to do. He has to move again—to a new city—and find a new home at the same time. If you're in Pinehurst,[68] you know the drill: new location—new life.

As Matthew puts it: *"Leaving Nazareth, Jesus went and lived in Capernaum,"* 20 mountainous miles—and a whole world—away from where He grew up.

And what about this new home for Jesus? Capernaum is a busy town on the northern shore of the Sea of Galilee. Fishing is big there, as you would expect, so big that fishermen move there from other places to compete in the market. And fishing—commercial fishing—requires boats, and boats have to be built and repaired, and that requires men who are skilled in woodworking. There's going to be a lot of work for carpenters.

Capernaum is also a commercial center—a transportation hub along the highway that goes to the Mediterranean in one direction and the Syrian capital, Damascus, in the other.

There's money to be made in Capernaum (honest and otherwise), and all kinds of people have moved there to get their share: Greeks, Romans, Persians—and Jews, of course—though

---

[66] Matthew 4:1-11.
[67] Matthew 4:12; Luke 4:16-30.
[68] Pinehurst, North Carolina, is a favorite retirement destination for many people who relocate from other parts of the country.

not the Jerusalem kind—not the religious and social elites. Capernaum is out there on a porous and perilous border—a working-class city with a frontier mentality.

Welcome to Capernaum, Mr. Jesus.

&

Jesus may be new in town, but it won't be long before people start to take notice. You see, Jesus didn't come to Capernaum to fit in, lay low or mind His own business. He doesn't really care about making a living. He might swing a hammer during the week to pay His bills, but on the Sabbath, He'll be in the synagogue, pounding away at something else: *"Repent, for the kingdom of heaven is near."*

It's simple—and sensational. And He's backing it up with mighty works: miracles of healing in a world without healthcare—miracles and a message that boggle the mind. God is breaking into this miserable world and making everything different. There is a power being unleashed into this world that nothing in this world can match—that no evil in this world can withstand.

And this power is present in the Person Who is proclaiming it—this new-in-town Carpenter named Jesus. God is right here! Not a million miles and a million wishes away—not separated from you by a million sins. God is not "way up there"—or "out there."

God is not even far enough away that you could call Him "the Man upstairs." He's not "upstairs." God is as close as the tip of your finger or the next beat of your heart—not the *idea* of God—the *reality*. The—*very*—God!

"The Man upstairs" is not upstairs; He's nearer, so much nearer, than that. He's so near, He's *here*.

But funny thing: He *is* a Man. Not a long-white-beard, old-as-dirt, kind of Man. More like a young, fairly average-looking Carpenter, building a few things and bringing the best news that anybody ever heard. God has come to us and has sent Himself as the Messenger to let us know it.

The New Guy in Town

"COMING TO A SYNAGOGUE NEAR YOU: Jesus, a new Carpenter in town; Jesus, God incarnate!"

It's kind of hard to get your mind around it—and you've had 2,000 years and all your life to get used to the idea. Think how the "Capernaumites" or "Capernaumanians" or whatever they called themselves, figured it the first time this Jesus stepped into the speaker's spot at the synagogue downtown.

"God is right here with you—and I am the Proof."

"How's that again?"

"The kingdom of heaven is near."

❧

And, absurd as that sounds, if you want to be able to believe it—let alone understand it—you're going to have to change your mind about some very basic and important things. Or as Jesus puts it: "Repent."

Yes, "repent" usually means "be sorry for doing something bad—or a lot of bad 'somethings.'"

But before you can do that, you're going to have to change your mind. You're going to have to change your mind about whether what you did was bad or not—and not whether it was bad according to some public standard of morality or social expectation—not whether other people think it was bad.

That only matters if you think people will treat you badly as a result of what they think.

And these days, most people are too tolerant to make a stink about somebody else's bad behavior.

No, when Jesus says "Repent," He means change your mind about what *you* think is right or wrong for *you*—how *you* judge what's good or bad for *you* to do—how you judge your *own* thoughts and actions.

That's much more basic, because inside—in your own heart—you decide good and bad *for you* in a whole different way. Inside, the questions center around your sense of survival and self-

From Matthew 4

preservation, securing for yourself the things you think you need, and things you want so badly you simply will not deny yourself, whatever it takes.

At that deep, personal level, everything is rationalized and justified. Your mind is made up and very hard to change. At that level, you *know* what you *know*. You have settled what is right and true—and real—for *you*. And if the very presence of God near you and next to you and in you is not real—it will require a radical change of mind to make it real—to you.

But suppose the presence of God is as real as Jesus says it is—not in your mind, but in Reality itself. You think God is nothing, or at least nowhere near, when He really is. You think God is nothing like what Jesus says He is, and God is *exactly* What and Who and where Jesus says He is.

What you think doesn't determine the reality of things—and especially not the reality of God. God is near or not, regardless of what you think. And Jesus says God *is* near—*present*—present in Jesus Himself, in fact. And if Jesus is right and you thought—think—otherwise, you will have to change your mind about that, and about everything else you believe *because* you believe that, because you have everything wrong—wrong about God—wrong about everything else in reality—wrong at every level for you.

If Jesus is right, your survival and self-preservation and security require a radically different perspective and approach, which can only be achieved by changing your mind about everything—repenting of everything you've done, which you did because of what you thought was reality.

You have to repent because everything you thought and believed was wrong.

Repent. See yourself and your actions and your understandings in light of the reality Jesus is presenting.

Repent. Agree with Jesus about the meaning of everything—in your life, and in the world around you.

Repent. And experience a relationship with God that you did not think was possible, but is.

If you don't repent, you won't see it. You won't see how remarkably, wonderfully close God is to you. You'll only see a very unremarkable looking Fellow making a fool of Himself by making the most absurd claims about God. You won't want to listen to Him or see Him because you will soon find His constant harping on this peculiar obsession of His tedious and offensive.

☙❧

But if you do listen to Jesus and change your mind enough to see the truth and reality of what He is saying, you will find yourself repenting over and over again, because your experience of the reality of an always present God will "open the eyes of your heart"[69] to all the other things you had wrong about God—and you—and your life. And you will change your mind about them, too. You will repent everything that needs to be repented as God shows you what it is.

When will you be done repenting?

When God has revealed everything you need to change your mind about.

But here's an interesting and encouraging thing: The repentance Jesus calls for begins in a sense of guilt or remorse or fear. Yet as this process of repentance continues over the course of your life, the growing experience of the reality of God's nearness and acceptance and support transforms your repentance into acts of increasing joy and relief.

Jesus simply says, *"Repent."*

Paul says, *"...be transformed by the renewing of your mind. Then you will be able to test and approve what God's will is—his good, pleasing and perfect will."*[70] It's the same thing, really.

---

[69] Paul Baloche, "Open the Eyes of My Heart," 2000.
[70] Romans 12:2, NIV.

Jesus didn't come to Capernaum—or here—to lay low or mind His own business.

And whether He's in here or out there, He's still pounding away at the same simple, spectacular truth: *"The kingdom of heaven is near.* God is here. If you don't believe it, you should. If you don't believe it, change your mind—starting now."

Welcome to our town, Mr. Jesus. Welcome to our church. Welcome to our lives and everything that means. Welcome, Mr. Jesus—glad You're here.

God's Wellness Plan

Matthew 4:23-25 ESV

To proclaim the good news of the kingdom of God, Jesus sometimes demonstrated what He meant by healing the sick. The Gospels tell of the different kinds of healings Jesus performed and that many came to Him to be healed.

[23] And [Jesus] went throughout all Galilee, teaching in their synagogues and proclaiming the gospel of the kingdom and healing every disease and every affliction among the people. [24] So his fame spread throughout all Syria, and they brought him all the sick, those afflicted with various diseases and pains, those oppressed by demons, those having seizures, and paralytics, and he healed them. [25] And great crowds followed him from Galilee and the Decapolis, and from Jerusalem and Judea, and from beyond the Jordan.

4.

God's Wellness Plan

Matthew 4:23-25 ESV

There was a time when to get sick was to die—to be injured was to be permanently disabled. There was a time when there were no ambulances to race to your house and take you to the hospital—and no hospitals for them to take you to. There was a time when medical men knew so little about the human body and the diseases that devoured it that anything they did was more likely to hurt you than help you—thus the first rule of medical care was a critical and necessary one: "Do no harm."[71]

And so to find a Man Who could restore the sick to health—Who could give the blind their sight back and put cripples on their feet—a Man Who cured everyone He touched, and killed no one—to find such a Man would be a miracle.

But the miracle is greater still: that Man did not wait to be found. He has come to find[72]—and heal—you. This Healer makes house calls.

Matthew says Jesus went throughout Galilee, teaching, preaching and healing. Galilee was filled with little villages, and no doubt the village folk would be impressed by any stranger who

---

[71] Attributed popularly to the Greek physician Hippocrates (c460BC-c370BC).
[72] Luke 19:10.

came to town with an interesting take on life-as-they-knew-it and the ability to express it well. But word was making its way as far north as Syria and as far south as Jerusalem about this new Guy in Galilee. They weren't talking about His teaching—that would come later.

The buzz was based on His ability to heal. And Matthew says the world came running—or more likely limping and crawling and being carried along by family and friends who recognized the chance of a lifetime when they heard the news: "There is a Healer in Galilee!" And they came from all over to be healed. First, Jesus went looking for them; then, they came looking for Him. They came looking because they had heard what Jesus could do.

How did Jesus heal? We don't really know. The Bible doesn't make much ado about His methods. Most of the time when He healed somebody, Jesus just touched the person.[73] Once or twice, He applied what the King James Version politely calls *"spittle."*[74] There were times when people touched Him and were healed,[75] and times when He just told people they were healed—and they were.[76]

What the Bible is very clear about is that Jesus healed people—a lot of people—with a lot of different diseases, ailments and injuries.[77] He had no stethoscope, no modern medicine, none of the dazzling array of technology essential to what healing is today. And yet, Jesus had the power to heal. There was apparently no medical malady He could not cure. Miraculous!

༄༅

But there were those Jesus did not heal. The Bible says Jesus did not heal those who did not believe He could heal them.[78] Not

---

[73] Matthew 8:3, 15.
[74] Mark 8:23; John 9:6.
[75] Matthew 9:20-21; 14:35-36.
[76] Matthew 8:5-13; Mark 10:46-52.
[77] Matthew 4:24.
[78] Matthew 13:54-58.

that He *would* not—not that He was offended by their attitude and decided to teach them "a lesson in manners" by not healing them. The skepticism, or downright disbelief, of people, even in His own hometown, *prevented* the healing miracles Jesus was willing, and otherwise able, to perform.

This must have made a significant impression on Jesus because later He would ask an invalid, *"Do you want to get well?"*[79] He asked a blind man, *"What do you want Me to do for you?"*[80] Another time He asked, *"Do you believe that I am able to do this?"*[81] Jesus believed—He knew for sure. But that was never the issue. It isn't clear whether faith was always required of the person or not, but it seems clear that a person could not actively dis-believe and still be healed.

But Jesus did heal enough people to build up a following of those who wanted to be "next." He could have gone into the healing business fulltime. People wanted—needed—to be healed. And someone with a genuine gift for healing was about as rare as God's Messiah in those days. Those who had money were willing to pay a lot of it to be healed.[82] And even today—with all the benefits of modern medicine at our beck and (911) call—we, too, would like to be healed—by Jesus. We come to Him—and bring others to Him—in prayer—beseeching Him—begging Him—to heal us.

And sometimes, He does. Sometimes, the answer to our prayers for healing is the supernatural miracle. Sometimes, Jesus answers with healing delivered by the methods of modern medicine. And sometimes, there is no healing, despite the best efforts of the best experts and the promise of the presence of the Holy Spirit.

Jesus did not heal every person who needed healing in His day, nor does He heal everyone who wants to be healed today. Jesus

---

[79] John 5:6.
[80] Matthew 20:32.
[81] Matthew 9:28.
[82] Mark 5:26-26.

did not go throughout Galilee—did not come into this world—simply to heal the sick. He is not called the Great Physician because He healed a few dozen, or a few hundred, or even a few thousand, sick people.

Jesus came to heal something far more serious and even more widespread than physical illness and injury. And His healing in Galilee and Jerusalem and wherever was a sign—a physical demonstration for those who live a physical existence—of the greater spiritual healing that is more important to God and more necessary for us.

Jesus healed the sick and still does, but that is only part of His work as the Great Physician. Matthew says Jesus was teaching in the synagogues and preaching the good news of the kingdom. That, too, was a part of the spiritual healing God desires to give. And when Jesus explained the deeper meaning of the scriptures of His people to the students of God's Word, and proclaimed a revelation that no one in the Old Testament had fully grasped, He was calling a world of sin-sick patients to the new and better life available beyond their spiritual illness.

But they could not just "get well," even with the best advice from the best wellness Source. So how was this spiritual healing to be accomplished?

Through a transfusion of sorts.

Paul says, *"Let this Spirit be in you that was in Christ Jesus."*[83] In a sense, Jesus inoculates us against the fatal effects of sin with a vaccination of His own shed blood. That's why Paul says, *"If Christ is in you, then even though your body is subject to death because of sin, the Spirit gives life because of righteousness."*[84]

---

[83] Philippians 2:5.
[84] Romans 8:10.

From Matthew 4

Yes, we're talking life and death here, but from a different perspective than that of your nearby medical center. Many people get well today who would surely have died in times past.

Many get well, but all of us die in the end. As we used to sing as children when we didn't know what it meant: "...upstairs, downstairs, we all fall down."[85]

"In Adam, all die."[86] As human beings, we will give up this physical life and discard these physical bodies and leave this world.[87] And because we are the children of Adam and Eve, we will have gotten sick spiritually before we do. Everyone suffers in this life, somewhere along the way. A little or a lot—sooner or later—the body feels the pain of life on its way to death.

But spiritual suffering can be greater and more dangerous, for the spiritual disease of sin is the only illness that will bring about a spiritual death and affect our eternal life.[88] And there is only One Who is able to heal the sickness and suffering of sin. The transfusion of God's Spirit into our hearts, and the application of Jesus' blood as the "antibiotic" for our sins, transforms us for living this life with a spirit healed and going from this life to the next in perfect peace.[89]

☙❧

Jesus went about healing every disease. When people realized what He was doing—what He was capable of doing—they brought the sick to Him—and He healed them.

And did you notice that His disciples were doing the same thing—healing the sick, restoring broken bodies and, with them, rebuilding broken souls? It's what His disciples do.[90]

---

[85] Traditional nursery rhyme popularly associated with the Black Death in Europe in 1665-1666.
[86] 1 Corinthians 15:22.
[87] Hebrews 9:27.
[88] Matthew 10:28.
[89] 2 Corinthians 1:22; Ephesians 1:7; Isaiah 26:3.
[90] John 14:12.

"But I can't do miracles! I can't heal the sick!"

Perhaps not, but you can bring the sick and the broken to the Great Physician Who can and does heal—even now. It's like being a certified "EST"—an "Emergency Spiritual Technician." Today, it is not enough to abide by the first rule of medicine: "Do no harm." People are suffering. People are dying. It is the chance of a lifetime. It may be their only chance.

He healed you. He can heal them.

He came to heal them.

Bring them to Jesus.

Matthew 5:1-12 ESV

When Jesus went up on a mountain to deliver what we know as the Sermon on the Mount, the people who heard Him were reminded of Moses bringing the Law of God to their ancestors from Mount Sinai. The Mosaic Law began with the Ten Commandments, the foundational requirements from which all other laws took their authority. The foundation of the Sermon on the Mount is a series of blessings, or beatitudes, in which Jesus reveals what the kingdom of God is like.

❦

¹ Seeing the crowds, [Jesus] went up on the mountain, and when he sat down, his disciples came to him.
² And he opened his mouth and taught them, saying:
³ "Blessed are the poor in spirit,
for theirs is the kingdom of heaven.
⁴ "Blessed are those who mourn,
for they shall be comforted.
⁵ "Blessed are the meek,
for they shall inherit the earth.
⁶ "Blessed are those
who hunger and thirst for righteousness,
for they shall be satisfied.
⁷ "Blessed are the merciful,
for they shall receive mercy.
⁸ "Blessed are the pure in heart,
for they shall see God.
⁹ "Blessed are the peacemakers,
for they shall be called sons of God.
¹⁰ "Blessed are those
who are persecuted for righteousness' sake,
for theirs is the kingdom of heaven.

¹¹ *"Blessed are you when others revile you*
 and persecute you
 and utter all kinds of evil against you falsely
 on my account.
¹² *Rejoice and be glad,*
 for your reward is great in heaven,
 for so they persecuted the prophets
 who were before you."

5.

Bizarre Blessings

Matthew 5:1-12 ESV

This year, we're "gonna" follow Jesus around the gospels like the fans have been following the golfers around Augusta National this week.[91] We're "gonna" gather reverently nearby whenever He stops, and watch in wonder when He does all those remarkable things we've heard about, and strain to hear every word He utters.

They say you should wear good shoes at Augusta if you're going to follow the players up the hills. The crowds followed Jesus up a hill in the Gospel of Matthew, and before the day was over, He had put on quite a show for them. The Bible says the crowds were *"amazed"* by His *"authority."*[92] He taught like nobody else. In golf terms, it was kind of like what Bobby Jones said of Jack Nicklaus one year at Augusta: He's "playing an entirely different game—a game with which I'm not familiar."[93]

When Jesus delivered His Sermon on the Mount, He introduced the spectators—and His devoted disciples—to an

---

[91] This sermon was preached on the Sunday of The Masters Golf Tournament, in Pinehurst, North Carolina, a small town that bills itself as "The Birthplace of American Golf."
[92] Luke 4:36, RSV.
[93] After Jack Nicklaus won the Masters in 1965.

entirely different reality—one with which they were wholly unfamiliar.

He introduced them to the kingdom of God—the kingdom that had arrived when He stepped onto the course we call "Earth." And we are still talking about His performance 2,000 years later.

We're going to go several rounds with the Sermon on the Mount over the next few weeks. Today, we start with the "front nine"—nine beatitudes—nine simple statements that seem at first glance to be like a lovely walk down a wide fairway. But don't get fooled by their familiarity. When you get into them, you'll find more there than you thought.

Those familiar with the Sermon on the Mount tend to take the beatitudes, not too *seriously*, but too *spiritually*. Jesus is very serious about what He has to say, but He is keeping His head down. He's looking at the world they—we—live in, every day. And the club He pulls out of His bag is "the beatitude."

Jesus didn't invent beatitudes. They're lying all over the Old Testament. Moses managed to fashion a few,[94] and the prophets pronounced a few more.[95] Beatitudes pop up here and there in Proverbs[96] and are scattered all over the Psalms.[97] *"Blessed are you when…"* they say. *"Blessed is the man who…"*

"Blessed?"

It means "fortunate"—so much so that you should be congratulated. It's not really to be "lucky," because luck doesn't play into it—it's not accidental. It's intentional—providential. Some Bibles translate the beatitudes as "happy," but that doesn't work, either, because as good as it is to be blessed, getting there may require you to "play through" some very *un*-happy territory.

"Blessed" is probably best, because it means that God is doing—or is going to do—something good for you, or to you. In

---

[94] Deuteronomy 7:14; 28:3-6.
[95] Isaiah 30:18; 56:1-2; Jeremiah 17:7.
[96] Proverbs 28:14; 29:18.
[97] Psalm 32:1; 33:12; 40:4; 84:4, etc.

the Old Testament, most beatitudes make sense because the reason God is going to do something good for the person in the beatitude is that the person is doing what God told him to do.

"Blessed is the man who fears the Lord."[98]
"Blessed are all who take refuge in him."[99]
"Blessed are those
   who walk in the light of your presence, Lord...[100]
   who don't walk in step with the wicked."[101]
"Blessed are those
   who act justly,
   who always do what is right."[102]
"Blessed is the one who is kind to the needy."[103]
"Blessed are those who have regard for the weak."[104]

You get the picture: do right—do good—get blessed. Blessed are the good. If you're righteous—congratulations! You're gonna get blessed. Master your long game. Master your short game. Be consistent, and you'll be a winner. Blessed are you when you deserve it.

Except that's not what Jesus says.

Sitting up there on the side of the mountain, getting ready to lay down the new law, Jesus doesn't congratulate the well-behaved, the deeply religious, or the spiritually mature. Who are the "winners" in this new kingdom of God?

If you can believe it, it's the spiritually *im*mature—the *poor* in spirit—or maybe just "the *poor*," if you take Luke's version[105] as the gospel truth.

---

[98] Psalm 112:1, ESV.
[99] Psalm 2:12, ESV.
[100] Psalm 89:15, NIV.
[101] Psalm 1:1, NIV.
[102] Psalm 106:3, NIV.
[103] Proverbs 14:21, NIV.
[104] Psalm 41:1, NIV.
[105] Luke 6:20.

Bizarre Blessings

All the Bible studies make the "poor in spirit" out to be the devotedly humble—those who are not proud of themselves because they know they have nothing to be proud of, apart from God. But maybe Jesus means what He says. Maybe He's talking about people who are just spiritually empty—bankrupt inside with nothing worth having to go on in their relationship with God, or anybody else, or themselves.

And then Jesus says: "Congratulations to the grief-stricken and miserable, the mourners. And hooray for the meek, all the little people who are always being run over by the big shots of the world. And 'How fortunate!' are the poor suckers who're starving for a little justice and can't ever seem to get a break—those who hunger and thirst for righteousness."

Or maybe Jesus is talking about all those people who couldn't do right if they tried, which some of them probably have, and even then, they still end up on the wrong side of the law—whether God's law or man's.

These are the people who are going to get blessed in God's kingdom?! It's like reading the will of some unbelievably rich philanthropist and learning that all his fortune goes to the panhandler at the corner, or the kid that sprayed graffiti all over the back fence, or the nutty neighbor next door.

"They don't deserve it! They don't deserve a penny!"

And that's why they're blest. It's bizarre, but there you have it. That's who's blest in God's kingdom. Go figure!

Jesus starts teaching about this kingdom of God that has come to earth and how you can be a citizen of the kingdom. And before He says anything about how to become a kingdom citizen, or what's expected of kingdom citizens, He tells what the King of the kingdom has already done for all the citizens.

Absolutely broke spiritually? No credit? No collateral? No co-signer?

No problem. Come on in.

From Matthew 5

Spiritually bankrupt?

Congratulations! The kingdom of heaven is yours.

Everything gone wrong in your life? Lost everything you ever cared about with no hope of ever getting it back? Dealing with despair and depression day in and day out?

Don't worry. God will mend your broken heart. God will restore your hope. God will pump out the grief and replace it with consolation, encouragement and joy.

God comforts the citizens of His kingdom. And in God's kingdom, the tables will be turned. The first shall be last and the last shall be first.[106] Those who figure out how to win on their own terms won't win anymore, in God's kingdom.[107] And those who never win, will never lose again. The whole world will be theirs, simply because God has chosen to give it to them.

In God's kingdom, the meek will inherit the earth. And those who want a little justice so bad they can almost taste it, but never seem to get a seat at the table to get that taste—those who always wanted to set a better example but couldn't—or never really wanted to after all—will. They will *be* right and *do* right. Those who hunger and thirst for righteousness will feast on it.

They will be filled with it—so filled with justice and righteousness that they and everybody else will be amazed at how different things are, and people are, in God's kingdom.

All this, Jesus promises before He says a word about what God requires of the citizens in the heavenly kingdom. All this is free gift, given before it's requested—given to those who deserve it least—to those least able—totally *un*-able, in fact—to repay the favor.

But once you become a citizen of the kingdom—once your life that was ruled and ruined by the world's sorrows is transformed by God's comfort—once you have been raised from "doormat" status to the place of importance God created you to occupy—

---

[106] Matthew 20:16.
[107] Mark 8:36.

once God has filled you to the brim with His righteousness, *then* what?

The bizarre blessings continue to flow. Citizenship in God's kingdom is a gift of grace—total, undeserved, spectacular, laugh-out-loud-at-your-good-fortune grace.[108]

And the citizen, by being a citizen in relationship with the King of the kingdom, begins to take on some small shadow of the characteristics of the King.[109] And though the citizen has no responsibility in transforming himself into the likeness of his Lord, he is rewarded again for the work of God in him.

It's like being paid an incredibly generous pension, and then having your boss match his own contributions, over and above what he paid for you. God is merciful—else there would be no kingdom for the likes of you and me to be citizens in.[110] And because we are in relationship with Him, we become merciful like Him. And He rewards us for that by showing us more mercy.

Because God is pure, perfect holiness,[111] we who are drawn into the atmosphere of His holiness in His kingdom take on some small measure of purity ourselves, and in the clearing away of the fog of sin and self-centeredness, we see in ourselves a clearer image of the One Who is the Source of the holiness in us.[112] We see God.

And this peacemaking thing? God made peace with us through Jesus Christ when we were still at war with Him.[113] And now that our war with God is over, we have been "repatriated," not to our home, but to His—to the place He prepared for us.[114]

---

[108] Ephesians 2:8-9.
[109] Philippians 3:10, 1 John 3:2.
[110] Ephesians 2:1-5.
[111] Leviticus 19:2; Isaiah 43:15.
[112] 2 Corinthians 7:1.
[113] Romans 5:1-8.
[114] Matthew 25:34; John 14:1-3; 1 Corinthians 2:9; Hebrews 11:16.

From Matthew 5

You see, citizens of God's kingdom are not merely citizens. All the citizens of God's kingdom are also members of the royal family of the kingdom—sons and daughters of the King.[115]

And, as such, we are His ambassadors, His trusted and valued representatives, sent to make peace between God and those who are still at war with Him, as we once were.[116]

And how fortunate we are to represent our King—our loving, merciful, gracious, Heavenly Father King— how fortunate we are to represent Him to those whose place in His kingdom is prepared, but who will not yet come.

In God's kingdom, Jesus says, the peacemakers are blest because they shall be called the sons and daughters of God. The truth is, we are blessed because we *are* the children of God,[117] and because of this exalted position God has given us, we are able to offer peace to others[118] and experience the added blessing that comes to *us* by being of some service to God in blessing *them*,[119] who like us, do not deserve it.

From the world's perspective, it is bizarre whom God chooses to bless. And even for us, it is bizarre that God should chose to bless us as He has.[120] But that's what they heard—all those who followed Jesus around and up the hill that day. And I feel very confident sharing this with you because, even though I do not know what color coat He wore (whether green or not), I have it on good authority that all those who followed Jesus around the Gospels called Him *"Master."*[121]

---

[115] Romans 8:14-17.
[116] 2 Corinthians 5:20.
[117] Matthew 5:9.
[118] 2 Corinthians 5:11, 18.
[119] Ephesians 4:11-13.
[120] 1 John 3:1.
[121] Matthew 8:19; 9:11; 12:38; 22:16, 24, 36; 26:49.

A Lesson in Prayer

Matthew 6:5-15 ESV

[Jesus said:]

⁵ "And when you pray, you must not be like the hypocrites. For they love to stand and pray in the synagogues and at the street corners, that they may be seen by others. Truly, I say to you, they have received their reward. ⁶ But when you pray, go into your room and shut the door and pray to your Father who is in secret. And your Father who sees in secret will reward you.

⁷ "And when you pray, do not heap up empty phrases as the Gentiles do, for they think that they will be heard for their many words. ⁸ Do not be like them, for your Father knows what you need before you ask him. ⁹ Pray then like this:

> "Our Father in heaven,
> hallowed be your name.
> ¹⁰ Your kingdom come,
> your will be done,
> on earth as it is in heaven.
> ¹¹ Give us this day our daily bread,
> ¹² and forgive us our debts,
> as we also have forgiven our debtors.
> ¹³ And lead us not into temptation,
> but deliver us from evil.

¹⁴ "For if you forgive others their trespasses, your heavenly Father will also forgive you, ¹⁵ but if you do not forgive others their trespasses, neither will your Father forgive your trespasses."

6.

A Lesson in Prayer

Matthew 6:5-15 ESV

"And when you pray…"
"But when you pray…"
"And when you pray…"

Did you hear Jesus in the Gospel reading? When Jesus turns His attention in the Sermon on the Mount to the subject of prayer, you get the sense that He just assumes that you pray. And He's right, of course. You pray. I pray. Everybody prays.

It's what you do when you're not God—when you remember you're not God—when you realize you need God.

Of course, that means you probably don't pray as often as you should or as well as you could. And because of that, you probably don't pray the way you would like to when you realize you really need to.

The disciples of Jesus prayed more than people usually do today. Ancient people were praying people—and the Jews more than most. They had prayers they knew by heart and they prayed them every day.

And still, Jesus taught His Jewish disciples how to pray. And He teaches His disciples to pray today.

A Lesson in Prayer

The most famous prayer Jesus taught His disciples we call "The Lord's Prayer." In Matthew, as you heard earlier, Jesus laid out, as part of the Sermon on the Mount, the words we're familiar with (except for the last part about "the kingdom and the power and the glory" being God's "forever and ever").

But in Luke's Gospel, Jesus offers up parts of the prayer in response to a request from one of His disciples, *"Lord, teach us to pray...."*[122]

And why did the disciple ask Jesus to teach them to pray?

According to Luke, he asked Jesus when Jesus had finished praying. The disciple wanted Jesus to teach him and his fellow disciples to pray because he and they had heard Jesus pray. And my suspicion is that it wasn't the first time they heard Jesus pray.

In fact, the Gospels—and Luke's Gospel in particular—reveal a Jesus Who was constantly, confidently, fervently, faithfully praying.[123] Unlike them—or us—Jesus did pray as often as He should have. And He prayed prayers as well as prayers could be prayed. So Who better to teach a lesson on prayer?

The first lesson is one of observation. *Watch* Jesus pray. Consider *when* He prays. Notice *why* He prays. Listen to *what* He says when the actual words are recorded. The Lord's Prayer is not the only model Jesus provided. It's not the only prayer you could pray.

They say Jesus *"often withdrew to lonely places and prayed"*[124] and *"spent the night praying to God"*[125]—that He *"fell with His face to the ground and prayed."*[126] Jesus was praying at His baptism, and *"the heavens opened before Him."*[127] He prayed on the Mount of

---

[122] Luke 11:1, RSV.
[123] Matthew 14:23; Luke 9:18; John 17.
[124] Luke 5:16, NIV.
[125] Luke 6:12, NIV.
[126] Matthew 26:39, NIV.
[127] Luke 3:21-22, NIV.

Transfiguration and *"the appearance of His face changed, and His clothes became as bright as a flash of lightning."*[128]

He prayed before He selected His 12 disciples[129] and then He prayed for them after that, to celebrate their successes,[130] and to protect them from their weaknesses.[131] Jesus prayed when healing the sick[132] and feeding multitudes.[133] He prayed for little children who were brought to Him[134] and for the people of Jerusalem who, like rebellious children, would *not* come to Him.[135] He prayed in the Upper Room[136] and in the Garden of Gethsemane[137] and on the Cross at Calvary.[138]

"Father, I thank you that you have heard me."[139]

"Father, glorify your name."[140]

"My Father, if it is not possible for this cup to be taken away unless I drink it, may your will be done."[141]

"I pray also for those who will believe in me...that all of them may be one, Father, just as you are in me and I am in you."[142]

"Father, forgive them, for they do not know what they are doing."[143]

"Father, into your hands I commit my spirit."[144]

❧❦

---

[128] Luke 9:28-35, NIV.
[129] Luke 6:12-13.
[130] Luke 10:17-21.
[131] Luke 22:32.
[132] Luke 5:12-16; Mark 7:32-37.
[133] John 6:11, Matthew 14:22-23.
[134] Matthew 19:13.
[135] Luke 19:41-44.
[136] Luke 22:17, 19.
[137] Mark 14:32-42.
[138] Matthew 27:46; Luke 23:34, 46; John 19:30.
[139] John 11:41, NIV.
[140] John 12:28, NIV.
[141] Matthew 26:42, NIV.
[142] John 17:20-21, NIV.
[143] Luke 23:34, NIV.
[144] Luke 23:46, NIV.

A Lesson in Prayer

You can learn a lot about something by watching somebody who knows what he's doing do it. And nobody knows prayer—or does prayer—better than Jesus.

But Jesus does more than "walk the walk." He also "talks the talk." Jesus doesn't just demonstrate proper and powerful prayer, He defines it and describes it so that those of us who don't come to it naturally can get the hang of it.

Before He gives His disciples those wonderful words to say in the Lord's Prayer, Jesus has a few things to say about the words and ways they *shouldn't* pray: *"And when you pray, do not be like the hypocrites, for they love to pray…to be seen by others.… And when you pray, do not keep on babbling like pagans, for they think they will be heard because of their many words."*

On the other hand, Jesus says,

"…pray so that you will not fall into temptation,"[145]

"…pray that you may be able to…stand before the Son of Man,"[146]

"…pray for those who mistreat you—who persecute you,"[147]

"Ask and it will be given to you; seek and you will find; knock and the door will be opened to you,"[148]

"If you believe, you will receive whatever you ask for in prayer."[149]

❦

And to keep the lesson interesting, Jesus illustrates prayer with parables.

"Then Jesus told his disciples a parable to show them that they should always pray and not give up"—the moral of the story being: *"…will not God bring about justice for his chosen ones, who cry out to him day and night?"*[150]

---

[145] Matthew 26:41, NIV.
[146] Luke 21:36, NIV.
[147] Matthew 5:44, Luke 6:28, NIV.
[148] Luke 11:9, NIV.
[149] Matthew 21:22, NIV.
[150] Luke 18:1, NIV.

From Matthew 6

Another time, Jesus said, *"Two men went up to the temple to pray, one a Pharisee and the other a tax collector. ...the tax collector stood at a distance. He would not even look up to heaven, but beat his breast and said, 'God, have mercy on me, a sinner.' I tell you that this man, rather than the other, went home justified before God."*[151]

Jesus painted an outlandish picture of parents giving their children snakes and scorpions instead of food to make the point that *"if you then, though you are evil, know how to give good gifts to your children, how much more will your Father in heaven give good gifts to those who ask him!"*[152]

So what has Jesus taught you about prayer?

Don't make a prayer a word longer than it has to be. Pray for real, not for show. Whenever and wherever you need to pray, pray. Pray for spiritual strength and support. Pray for moral courage. Pray with humility. Pray with gratitude. Pray with unflagging determination. Pray with unwavering confidence. Pray for what you need. Pray for what others need. Pray for those who need to get off your back. Pray for their forgiveness and their wellbeing, because *you* have been forgiven and healed of everything that stood in the way of your saving relationship with the God to Whom *you* pray.

Pray with your words and with God's words. No amount of human eloquence is sufficient to impress God, while the clumsiest, totally tongue-tied attempt at prayer will never frustrate or weary God, because as Paul says, every prayer you pray—or try to pray—becomes the perfect prayer of the Holy Spirit to the Father on your behalf.[153]

---

[151] Luke 18:9-14, NIV.
[152] Matthew 7:11, NIV.
[153] Romans 8:26-27.

A Lesson in Prayer

"*And when you pray…*" says Jesus, "*This, then, is how you should pray*:

"*Our Father who art in heaven…*" Just like a letter or an email, put the right address on your prayer. Send it where it needs to go. And know Who It is that waits to receive it, and the spirit in which it will be received. Your prayer will not be an imposition on a stranger. It is invited and eagerly anticipated by a loving Father, the One in Whom all the good and best characteristics of our understanding of fathers is fulfilled in perfect fullness.

"*Hallowed be your name. Your kingdom come. Your will be done on earth as it is in heaven.*" Put yourself in your proper place in relationship with your Heavenly Father. Be the one who rightly worships Him. Align your will, your dreams, your hopes and desires with the Father's, knowing that only in His kingdom can you live secure—only in His will will you find the ultimate and permanent good you seek, without success, anywhere else.[154]

"*Give us this day our daily bread.*" Of all the possessions you could want, and all that you have pursued, ask only for what you need, for nothing that you possess is better than the life that your Heavenly Father has given and daily sustains. It is God Who gives the grain, and the ground that will grow it, and the rain that will raise it up out of His good earth.[155] But for grain to become bread it must pass through human hands, the hands of neighbors, often unknown, who every day share with God in giving to you the gift of life.

"*And forgive us our trespasses, as we forgive those who trespass against us*"…for no matter what you possess, you do not possess the perfect balance sheet, free of wrongs that you've done to others or of injuries received at others' hands. But to clear the debts from your side of the ledger, you must constantly clear the other side, quickly giving the mercy and grace to others that you need and desire yourself.

---

[154] Isaiah 26:3.
[155] Leviticus 26:4; Deuteronomy 11:11-14; Joel 2:23; Zechariah 10:1.

From Matthew 6

"And lead us not into temptation, but deliver us from evil..." for experience—painful, shameful experience—has shown that you cannot withstand for long the moral testing of this life. Your only path to victory over evil is to be carried over it and away from it by One Who is not subject to its seductive, destructive power.

And as for "the kingdom, and the power and the glory" being God's—"forever and ever"—well, Jesus didn't give us that part in the lesson. That affirmation came later by way of the Holy Spirit Who taught it to the Church that grew up in the shadow of the Cross. But for 1,900 years and more, we've been praying the Lord's Prayer this way.

And there probably hasn't been a day since Jesus taught it that somebody somewhere wasn't praying it. And since Jesus first started teaching that prayer to that first dozen disciples, the class has grown from dozens to hundreds to thousands to millions to hundreds of millions, all praying as Jesus taught: the Lord's Prayer and millions more prayers every day, in more words and languages than anybody could keep up with.

You see, Jesus wasn't teaching those disciples (or you) a prayer—He was, and is, teaching you to pray—everywhere—everyday—so that you may be in constant contact and continuous conversation[156] with the God Who made you and sent Jesus to save you—the God Who will always be your Father Who is in heaven and Whose kingdom has come on earth, from whence your prayers rise up to Him.

And in that assurance, we are bold to pray: *"Our Father...."*

---

[156] 1 Thessalonians 5:17.

The Problem with Prosperity

Matthew 6:24-34 NRSV

[Jesus said:]

²⁴ "No one can serve two masters; for a slave will either hate the one and love the other, or be devoted to the one and despise the other. You cannot serve God and wealth.

²⁵ "Therefore I tell you, do not worry about your life, what you will eat or what you will drink, or about your body, what you will wear. Is not life more than food, and the body more than clothing? ²⁶ Look at the birds of the air; they neither sow nor reap nor gather into barns, and yet your heavenly Father feeds them. Are you not of more value than they? ²⁷ And can any of you by worrying add a single hour to your span of life? ²⁸ And why do you worry about clothing? Consider the lilies of the field, how they grow; they neither toil nor spin, ²⁹ yet I tell you, even Solomon in all his glory was not clothed like one of these. ³⁰ But if God so clothes the grass of the field, which is alive today and tomorrow is thrown into the oven, will he not much more clothe you—you of little faith? ³¹ Therefore do not worry, saying, 'What will we eat?' or 'What will we drink?' or 'What will we wear?' ³² For it is the Gentiles who strive for all these things; and indeed your heavenly Father knows that you need all these things. ³³ But strive first for the kingdom of God and his righteousness, and all these things will be given to you as well.

³⁴ "So do not worry about tomorrow, for tomorrow will bring worries of its own. Today's trouble is enough for today."

7.

The Problem with Prosperity

Matthew 6:24-34 NRSV

Today marks the end of my "weekend warrior" status here, driving down for the services and heading back to Virginia after. Next weekend, when I come down, I will be staying. I have been issued keys to the building and a mail slot in the Church Office, so it's beginning to seem "real."

Already, I feel like I've had an interesting initiation of sorts into the preaching rotation. Two weeks ago, I drew Mothers' Day and Pentecost Sunday. Today, it's Memorial Day and "Difficult-Passage-from-the-Lectionary" Sunday. Memorial Day you're familiar with, and the words of Jesus about the place of property or possessions or money in our lives should not be completely unknown, even if they are not the most comforting in the Bible.

If there is a common thread running between the civic holiday and the sacred text, it may be the business of service. So let's pull that thread for a moment.

Today, many Christian congregations are honoring the service of current and former members of our armed forces. The recognition is deserved, of course, but unlike Veterans' Day in November, Memorial Day was intended to focus our attention on

The Problem with Prosperity

a more select subset of America's servicemen and women: those who actually died defending their country.

Whether killed by enemy fire, accident, or disease, those who gave their "last full measure of devotion"[157]—their very lives—in the service of their country are the proper subject of our attention and appreciation this weekend. Millions have given their lives for this country across its 233 years of history, and more are doing so today. Because they are gone, their families, their friends, their comrades and their nation must make the effort to remember them.

But the sacrifice they made—the *ultimate* sacrifice—is one that all servicemen and women are asked to make—expected to make—if circumstances require. Every service member swears an oath when joining up to submit to higher authorities and obey their orders, even if doing so will cost them their lives.

Not everyone who takes that oath is really prepared to give his life for his country. Most don't expect to ever face that prospect—and fortunately, most won't.

But many who take the oath are not even prepared for the other, more common sacrifices required by life in the military. They don't really know what "service" means. But don't worry, the military will teach them. The military will make demands on them they never experienced before.

For instance, even when they are away from their appointed place of duty, the military will lay claim to their lives and impose its authority over them. It will enforce its pre-eminence over any other claimant for their time and attention—and service—if it so chooses.

Military people may work other jobs—serve other employers—if off-duty time permits. I am doing so myself for the next few months.[158] But were the military to call them back (which,

---

[157] A line from Abraham Lincoln's *Gettysburg Address*, November 19, 1863.
[158] I began my service to this church while on "terminal leave" from the Navy, using up several months of leave I had earned and not used before retiring.

in my case, it will not), there would be no question of which employer has the pre-eminent claim on the service member's life. He is obligated to fulfill his military responsibilities—whatever they may turn out to be—whenever they are in conflict with civilian commitments...

༺༻

...which brings us to the business on the mind of Jesus in the sixth chapter of Matthew, right in the middle of His Sermon on the Mount.

Jesus is also dealing with the difficulty of divided loyalties, the unacceptable conflict of competing commitments. The contrast for Jesus is not between military service and civilian work, but between submission to God and submission to something called "mammon."

"Mammon" is one of those special words in the Bible they didn't even bother to translate from the Aramaic that Jesus actually spoke into the Greek of the New Testament. But everybody who spoke Aramaic knew what Jesus meant: "Mannon" meant money, or property, or material wealth.

Jesus said, *"You cannot serve both God and mammon,"* according to my translation of the Bible. Unfortunately, my translation is a little too polite here, because what Jesus actually says is, *"You cannot **be the slave of** God and mammon."*

A servant may serve, if he so chooses, but a slave is the property of his owner. A slave is totally and completely possessed. The idea of a shared ownership of a slave—of a slave's divided obedience to multiple masters—is a logical impossibility. That's why Jesus says you "*can*-not," rather than you "*should* not." By the same logic, no one should make another person his slave because then the one who would "own" the other person puts himself in competition with God Who alone has the rightful claim of ownership over every person (by virtue of His having created us.)

The Problem with Prosperity

But that's getting a little complicated, and it's not really where Jesus is going with this, so let's back up and pick up His trail.

According to Jesus, although it is not possible to be the slave of both God and material wealth at the same time, it is possible to be the slave of either. Of course we can be possessed by God—and want to be (or, at least, we say we do). But we can also be possessed by our possessions. We can become the slaves of material things.

That was the point Jesus was making in the parable of the prosperous farmer in Luke, Chapter 12.[159] There a man had become so consumed with the accumulation of wealth that he became morally, socially and spiritually bankrupt. When he was congratulating himself for attaining everything he could imagine, he was actually losing everything that mattered.[160]

So is God against money? Does God oppose prosperity? Let us hope not, for ours is a prosperous church. And many of us have enjoyed great prosperity, by any objective standard.

Fortunately, Jesus is not saying that "mammon"—material wealth—prosperity—is evil. But He *is* saying that it is dangerous. The problem with prosperity is our natural human desire for it—a desire that, if not controlled, can enslave us. That's why the Bible says that *"the love of money"* (rather than money itself) *"is the root of all evil."*[161]

The issue is as much about subjective perspective as objective reality. The problem with prosperity can affect the "have nots" as well as the "haves."

If you become fixated on obtaining a measure of prosperity you do not have, the desire alone can enslave you without ever providing you the material benefits you crave. Not everyone to whom Jesus was preaching was prosperous.

---

[159] Luke 12:16-21.
[160] Matthew 16:26.
[161] 1 Timothy 6:10.

But some of them surely were. Zacchaeus had made a fortune with his tax-collection racket.[162] And at least one rich young ruler asked Jesus for advice.[163] Both had more "mammon" than you could shake a diversified portfolio at, and both were enslaved to it.

The problem with Zacchaeus' prosperity was in how he acquired it. To gain wealth, he had cheated and extorted money from those who had far less than he. For "the almighty dollar"— or *dinarii* (the money of his day)—he had destroyed relationships and broken the moral code that bound God's people to one another as family. Prosperity had become his god as he became an outcast in his own hometown.

Nothing is said against the way the rich young ruler acquired his wealth. Let us assume the process of "wealth accumulation" was, for him, above reproach. The problem with this fellow's prosperity was not how he gained it, but his fear of losing it. However he got it, he could not let anything compete with his keeping it. When offered a stake in the start-up of Jesus' salvation-of-the-world (and the young man's soul) venture, the rich young ruler had to pass up this once-in-a-lifetime opportunity because "preserving his capital" was more important. His earthly prosperity had become a problem of eternal proportions.

What is the common thread in "the prosperity problem"? Whether you *don't* have it and *want* it—are doing *whatever* it takes to *get* it—or are *afraid* of *losing* it—prosperity will become your substitute and wholly insufficient god, if you allow it to become your "treasure."

Earlier in the sixth chapter of Matthew, the Gospel reading for today, Jesus said, *"Do not lay up for yourselves treasures on earth, where moth and rust consume and where thieves break in and steal, but lay up for yourselves treasures in heaven, where neither moth nor rust consumes and where thieves do not break in and steal. For where your treasure is, there will your heart be also."*

---

[162] Luke 19:1-10.
[163] Matthew 19:16-30; Luke 18:18-30.

The Problem with Prosperity

As usual, Jesus goes to the heart of the matter. And the heart of the matter regarding prosperity is what your heart treasures most of all. Are the material possessions you have—or want to have—the most important things in your measure of the meaning of your life? Or have you ordered your priorities according to a different plan? The desire to have—or the fear of losing—the things of this world will enslave you to a lesser god. And the fruit of this allegiance to the god of earthly treasure is an anxiety about life that no amount of material prosperity will ever fully overcome. And all the while, the true and all-sufficient God is providing for all the needs of His children *"exceeding abundantly."*[164]

Prosperity is not evil. But it is dangerous. The danger is moral and spiritual, as well as emotional and psychological. But Jesus knows how to avoid that danger and has been kind enough to reveal the secret to us: *"Seek ye first the kingdom of God and his righteousness,"* Jesus says, *"and all these things shall be added unto you."*

To avoid the problem of this world's material prosperity, make the spiritual prosperity that God provides a higher priority—the highest priority of all.

Jesus says the slave of mammon is anxious about life, asking, *"What shall we eat? What shall we drink? What shall we wear?"*

Spiritual prosperity, based on a confidence in God's providential care, is able to say, *"I have learned in whatsoever circumstance I find myself, therewith to be content."*[165]

That's the thread of the argument, as I understand it.

What is your greatest treasure today? Where is your heart?

Earth or heaven?

God or mammon?

Whose slave are you?

---

[164] Ephesians 3:20, KJV.
[165] Philippians 4:11, KJV.

8.

Will You Give Them Stones?

Matthew 7:7-11 and Joshua 4:1-9 RSV

Jesus had some important things to say about children—and about parenting. Some of what He has to say is woven into the Sermon on the Mount. Here's Matthew, Chapter 7, verses 7 through 11.

❧

⁷ "Ask, and it will be given you; seek, and you will find; knock, and it will be opened to you. ⁸ For every one who asks receives, and he who seeks finds, and to him who knocks it will be opened. ⁹ Or what man of you, if his son asks him for bread, will give him a stone? ¹⁰ Or if he asks for a fish, will give him a serpent? ¹¹ If you then, who are evil, know how to give good gifts to your children, how much more will your Father who is in heaven give good things to those who ask him!"

❧

When Jesus says to His mostly male audience, *"Which of you, if his son asks for bread, will give him a stone?"* the answer appears obvious. Any decent parent would be quick to respond: "I love my child. I wouldn't give him a stone!" Only a cruel, twisted mind would think of giving a child a useless piece of rock when his little stomach is empty. The point of the question is clear: You can depend on your Heavenly Father to meet your needs.

But what if a stone represented more than "a useless piece of rock"? Listen to another story, this time from Joshua, Chapter 4, verses 1 through 9.

☙❧

When all the nation had finished passing over the Jordan, the LORD *said to Joshua,* ² *"Take twelve men from the people, from each tribe a man,* ³ *and command them, 'Take twelve stones from here out of the midst of the Jordan, from the very place where the priests' feet stood, and carry them over with you, and lay them down in the place where you lodge tonight.'"* ⁴ *Then Joshua called the twelve men from the people of Israel, whom he had appointed, a man from each tribe;* ⁵ *and Joshua said to them, "Pass on before the ark of the* LORD *your God into the midst of the Jordan, and take up each of you a stone upon his shoulder, according to the number of the tribes of the people of Israel,* ⁶ *that this may be a sign among you, when your children ask in time to come, 'What do those stones mean to you?'* ⁷ *Then you shall tell them that the waters of the Jordan were cut off before the ark of the covenant of the* LORD*; when it passed over the Jordan, the waters of the Jordan were cut off. So these stones shall be to the people of Israel a memorial for ever."*

⁸ *And the men of Israel did as Joshua commanded, and took up twelve stones out of the midst of the Jordan, according to the number of the tribes of the people of Israel, as the* LORD *told Joshua; and they carried them over with them to the place where they lodged, and laid them down there.* ⁹ *And Joshua set up twelve stones in the midst of the Jordan, in the place where the feet of the priests bearing the ark of the covenant had stood; and they are there to this day.*

☙❧

What if a stone was a timeless, visible reminder of a people's life-changing encounter with Almighty God? For Joshua and the children of Israel, this was the case 12 times over as they crossed the Jordan River to take possession of the Promised Land. Twelve strong men shouldered the weight of 12 great stones as this new

From Matthew 7

nation walked through a miracle. And when that special moment in time was over, the stones remained as a witness to the day when a people walked with God between the waters—and lived!

If we could speak symbolically of a stone as the "souvenir" of God's divine involvement in our human experience—if we could use the word "stone" with the meaning Joshua found in it—perhaps Jesus would not mind if we took another look at His apparently rhetorical question.

You see, this is a question of greatest importance for us today: Bread or stones?

Your children ask for "bread." That is, they have physical needs like adults, yet they aren't yet able to meet those needs by themselves. They depend on you—they trust you—to provide what they need.

But as we read in the Book of Joshua, children also ask about "stones." Their hunger for food and physical nourishment is often equaled, and occasionally surpassed, by their curiosity and hunger for spiritual understanding. And again, they depend on and trust you, their parents, to provide.

Now parents must certainly meet the physical needs of their children. Boys and girls must be fed and clothed and housed. Nothing is so disgusting as a mother or father who will not fulfill this obligation—who abuses this sacred trust. Nothing is so pitiful as the despair of a mother or father who does not have the means to feed his or her children, or treat their illnesses, or give them a home. And the world has far too many parents in both categories.

Some here today are of that generation that watched parents work long and hard during the Great Depression to provide the barest of necessities when many in this country could not feed themselves. A younger generation grew up with parents whose attitudes and values were shaped by living through those terrible years of uncertainty and sacrifice. Within just about every one of us, then, is a strong commitment to giving our children what we couldn't have—to giving them "bread"—meeting their material requirements—and their wants.

We also pay a lot of attention to their social needs, and their educational needs, and their psychological and emotional needs. We bend over backwards and go the second (and third) mile to ensure that our sons and daughters experience the best of everything our efforts and our incomes can provide.

And yet, other words of Jesus seem to echo faintly in the recesses of our minds: *"Man does not live by bread alone."*[166]

"But bread is important!"

Yes, it is, but not *all*-important.

Remember the setting of these words of Jesus? Our Lord had gone into the Wilderness, not eating for many days. Then He faced a battle of wills with the devil, who said, "Why don't You turn these stones into bread?" "Stones are important, are they? Do away with them. Direct all your attention and energy to making bread."

Now, the land of Israel is not a very big place—maybe the size of New Hampshire. And as Jesus went up into its mountainous wilderness, struggling with Satan's great temptations, Jesus could look out over the miles to the Jordan River, just as some of you have scanned the distant horizon from the Blue Ridge or some other mountains range. Jesus could have looked out over the Jordan River that flowed along to the south, past a little village called Gilgal. And perhaps Jesus (being a Jew and well-versed in the sacred scriptures) remembered at that moment the times when He asked His father, Joseph, or read in the Bible as we have read in ours today: *"What do these stones mean?"*

And Jesus said to Satan, "Bread isn't everything."

While you work to meet the material needs and wants of your children, are you ignoring or neglecting or shortchanging their spiritual needs? God had Joshua erect that monument of stones, not for the people who crossed the Jordan that day, but for their

---

[166] Matthew 4:4, NET.

From Matthew 7

children, and for the children who would follow after them, generation after generation.

And if the stones at Gilgal were a timeless symbol of God's presence and help in the lives of His people, *where are your stones—your* timeless evidence of God's hand in the affairs of *your* life?

The question you must ask yourself as a parent is not, "If my child asks for bread, will I give her a rock?" but rather, "If my child asks for a 'stone'—a symbol of my encounter with God—will I try to distract him with bread?" When your child is asking questions of spiritual importance to him or her—whether openly, or silently in that active little mind—will you address your child's spiritual need honestly and effectively? Or will you try to avoid those questions with more attention to supplying "goods and services"? So many of us try to give our children everything they want, and then wonder why they are neither happy nor satisfied.

The answer is "spiritual mal-nourishment." "Bread" is perishable" while "stone" endures. Bread meets the needs of the moment while the kind of stone we are talking about meets the needs of eternity. "Stone" suggests substance, strength and security. We sing, "On Christ, the solid Rock, I stand."[167] There are some essentials that money just can't buy, and some hungers that no bread will satisfy.

In those critical and important moments of your life, when God sends His Holy Spirit to take an active part, there ought to be some "marker" to show that God was in that experience. There ought to be a reminder to which your children can point and say, "What does that mean?"

"Why do you pray, Daddy?"

"Why do you read the Bible every day, Mommy?"

"Why do we go to church all the time?"

"Why do we put so much money in the offering plate?" (Remember, of course, that it doesn't take much money to impress

---

[167] Edward Mote, "My Hope is Built on Nothing Less," 1834.

a little child; many think a nickel is worth more than a dime because it's bigger.)

"Why don't you get upset and say ugly words when things don't go the way you want them to?"

"What do these stones mean?"

❧❧

Sometimes Navy chaplains are assigned to Marine Corps units. I began my career assigned to the Second Marine Division at Camp Lejeune in North Carolina. During that tour, my battalion deployed for six months, and on my daughter's second birthday, I was "deposited" with my troops on a beach in Oman (a small country on the Arabian Peninsula).

We were not allowed to take pictures (for security reasons) and there were no shops or markets in this deserted region of the coastline from which to buy souvenirs. The only reminder—the only evidence— of my experience there I could bring home was a collection of uniquely shaped rocks I gathered along the shore. And I carried those rocks halfway-round the world for my daughter to see. Those rocks showed her where I had been and what it had been like for me there.

Now the stones of Joshua we read about in the Bible were not little rocks easily plucked from the dry riverbed in passing, but great stones carried with supreme physical effort and spiritual dedication. The stones were carried to tell of deliverance from danger and despair.

What about those times when you faced situations that threatened to overwhelm you like a raging flood, and instead God seemed to part the waters and bring you through? Yes, you may wear the wrinkles or bear the scars from it, but these may be the very symbolic stones to which a boy or girl can point and say, "What does that mean?" And if the symbols—the monuments— are there, can you tell your children what they mean about God and your relationship with Him?

From Matthew 7

You know, in the fourth chapter of Joshua there are actually two accounts of setting up these stones. In the second account, the children are to ask, *"What do these stones mean **to you**?"* That's really what your children want to know. They aren't interested in *theology*; they want to hear your *testimony*! They want to look at you and see "a beacon to God, to faith and loyalty."[168]

A professor of mine once asked our class, "What do you know about God that you haven't read somewhere or heard from someone else?"

That's what every child is asking every mother and father. Your children are looking into your heart, looking for the God Who lives and reigns—looking to see if He lives and reigns there in *your* heart. Your children want to discover that God from the spiritual monuments you have erected to Him through your faith, your character and your lifestyle.

Your children are on a great spiritual quest of discovery. Their lives and their eternity, and those of their children and grandchildren beyond them, will be shaped and formed by what they find. You, more than anyone else, must provide the markers and the milestones—and the monuments—along their way. If your children ask you for bread, then give them bread.

But if they ask for stones....

---

[168] Earl Marlatt, "Are Ye Able," (Refrain), 1926.

Just Ask

James 1:2-8 ESV

² Count it all joy, my brothers, when you meet trials of various kinds, ³ for you know that the testing of your faith produces steadfastness. ⁴ And let steadfastness have its full effect, that you may be perfect and complete, lacking in nothing.
⁵ If any of you lacks wisdom, let him ask God, who gives generously to all without reproach, and it will be given him. ⁶ But let him ask in faith, with no doubting, for the one who doubts is like a wave of the sea that is driven and tossed by the wind. ⁷ For that person must not suppose that he will receive anything from the Lord; ⁸ he is a double-minded man, unstable in all his ways.

Matthew 7:7-11 ESV

[Jesus said:]
⁷ "Ask, and it will be given to you; seek, and you will find; knock, and it will be opened to you. ⁸ For everyone who asks receives, and the one who seeks finds, and to the one who knocks it will be opened. ⁹ Or which one of you, if his son asks him for bread, will give him a stone? ¹⁰ Or if he asks for a fish, will give him a serpent? ¹¹ If you then, who are evil, know how to give good gifts to your children, how much more will your Father who is in heaven give good things to those who ask him!"

9.

Just Ask

James 1:2-8; Matthew 7:7-11 ESV

The part of the Bible you heard today says, *"Count it all joy...when you meet trials of various kinds...."* If you take that advice seriously, some of you ought to be absolutely ecstatic!

Do hard times make for happy hearts?

Hardly!

Nobody in his right mind wants hardship, suffering, grief or stress. If we were to pray for what we really want, it would probably sound more like the Marti Gras mantra: "Let the *good* times *roll!*"

But they don't—not always. And sometimes, good times seem absent all together. To "count" the bad times—or even the normal times—as "all joy" would seem to require a different kind of calculator than most people carry around with them.

Fortunately, it's not the times—whether good, bad or indifferent—that we are to rejoice in as Christians. It is the trials of various kinds our experiences contain.

What is James talking about?

It is the spiritual version of "No pain, no gain." There is in every difficult circumstance—every physical illness or injury—every financial setback—every political crisis—every interpersonal conflict—every moral challenge—every "dark night of the soul"[169]—a spiritual trial—a test of your faith.

Now let me make a distinction before I go on. James is talking about testing—not temptation. The devil tempts you. God does not.

Temptation is the stimulation of our human desires to do what we want to do when we should not, or to avoid doing what we should do when we don't want to. Temptation is the psychological, physical or social pressure to be selfish instead of self-less, to go the easy way that's wrong instead of the hard way that's right. Temptation is the urge to put your agenda above God's.

God does not tempt you. He does not try to get you to do what He does not want you to do.

※

But God does test you—every day—all the time. In everything you experience, good and bad, there is a divine test. In every temptation—that God does not send—there is also a test for you that He does set up.

It is not that God fancies pop quizzes to put you on the spot and prove what you're lacking. God allows everything to be a test of your faith so that in confronting the challenge, you have the opportunity to have your faith strengthened. It is like the athlete who runs till it hurts and them pushes herself through the pain so that she may build her stamina and increase her speed. It is like the body-builder who forces the heavy weights away from his chest, despite the discomfort, so that the muscles there and throughout his body will grow more powerful. These are physical trials. And there are spiritual trials that function the same way: to strengthen us.

The first thing James does in his whole letter is point out this remarkable truth about adversity that all of us are inclined to miss

---

[169] A phrase made famous by the Spanish friar, St. John of the Cross, in his poem, *The Dark Night*, written c. 1578.

From Matthew 7

as we struggle under pressure or endure pain: God uses everything you experience to make you stronger in faith. And in the midst of all your hardships, that's a truth worth celebrating!

But before you break out the party hats and noise-makers, you need to know another very important part of this process. Your hardships and heartaches do not *automatically* strengthen your faith. Every trial you undergo in life does not come with a *guaranteed* verdict in your favor. You can be strengthened by your trials. God wants you to be strengthened, which is why He arranges for every hard thing you face to contain within it a way to grow closer to Him and more like Jesus.

But you do not *have to* be strengthened. You can also be weakened—significantly—fatally. But we'll come back to that later.

❧

For now, let's focus on the business of strengthening your faith—of passing God's test.

It says that passing the spiritual test embedded in our trials produces steadfastness. Steadfastness.

That's a rather uncommon word in our culture today. It is a commodity not much in demand by those determined to have everything that everybody thinks is worth having.

So, is steadfastness worth the hassle of trying to pass the tests of life in the modern world? What is steadfastness?

Steadfastness is strength of a particular kind. It means the ability to endure great weight—to carry heavy loads. It is a calm courage born of facing down that which engenders great fear. It is the peaceful assurance that you can withstand the storm because you have withstood others before. Steadfastness is the ability and the willingness to go one more lap around the track of life when everybody else has nothing left—to go one more round with the troubles of this world that are determined to "do you in," knowing you will be all right in the end.

Steadfastness builds on itself. It is, itself, strengthened and increased with every trial you successfully endure. It is possible to reach a place of full effect where your steadfastness has become perfect and complete.

But how do you get there? How do you make your trials more than just the misery you would rather avoid?

I thought you would never ask. (And, unfortunately, far too many never do.)

The secret to overcoming the impact of hardships and loss, and to finding joy in the midst of misery, is to see in all things—including, and especially, the negative things—the opportunity to call upon the Lord for the help you need. All you have to do is ask.

"If any of you lacks wisdom," says James, *"let him ask...."* If you do not know how to handle some hardship, ask for the wisdom to see the proper response. If you do not know what some difficulty means—or how you got messed up in it—ask for the wisdom to understand your dilemma and what you should do about it. Ask for the insight to be able to endure it, until you can get out of it, if that's possible—or as long as you must, however long that must be.

James might just as well have added: "If anyone lacks courage, let him ask," or "If anyone lacks strength, let him ask," or "If anyone lacks ability, let him ask." Even, "If anyone lacks faith, let him ask." I seem to recall a father in the Bible at the end of his hope who cried out, *"I believe! Help my unbelief!"*[170]

But here is a crucial, though frequently overlooked, point: When you ask, "Ask God."

The divine test in every difficulty is simply this: Will you ask God for the help you need, or try to "tough it out" on your own? Who do you trust most to help you—to "save" you?

Don't try to impress God with how self-reliant you are. "No thanks, God. I got this one."

---

[170] Mark 9:17-27, RSV.

From Matthew 7

Self-reliance fails God's test, every time. Even if you're sure you "got it," you might just want to ask God for help anyway, just in case you've totally underestimated the situation, which is so terribly easy to do.

And you should know: The steadfastness that trials produce is not your doing. It is the miracle that God works in you when you ask Him to guide you and protect you in the shadowy valleys through which you walk in this life. If you "fear no evil" for any other reason than that "His rod and His staff" are comforting you, you've got a lot more to be afraid of than the evil.[171]

God uses every trial you face to force you to make a choice between complete submission to His power and authority and grace, or misplaced trust in yourself or anybody else.

To pass God's test, you have to count on God, if you are to *"count it all joy."*

༺•༻

Now, James didn't come up with this pearl of wisdom by himself, of course. Jesus told the multitude listening to His Sermon on the Mount: *"Ask, and it will be given to you.... For everyone who asks receives...."*

And then Jesus went on to assure His listeners that they could pray with complete confidence, not because of how impressive or moving their prayers were, but because of the completely dependable character of God.

"If you then, who are evil, know how to give good gifts to your children, how much more will your Father Who is in heaven give good things to those who ask Him!"

The point, as James put it, is this: *"...ask in faith, with no doubting...."* This was not a casual invitation to participate in a theoretical exercise; it was a serious call to intensely practical application. These were people who were facing *"trials of various*

---

[171] Psalm 23:4.

kinds" every day. He addressed them as "the dispersed"—"the scattered." They had been driven from their homes because of their belief in Jesus. They suffered physical, financial, social and political persecution for their commitment to Christ. And they would suffer more. Their trials were far from over.

But it was not just suffering. These were not just hardships—unjustified trials that served no purpose. God gave their suffering a purpose. He gave their trials meaning. God used what they went through to make them more like Jesus—to draw them closer to Him. He made them steadfast in their faith and enabled them to use their suffering to win others to Christ and change the world.

You and I are here today because men and women we will never know this side of heaven asked God in faith for the ability to endure their trials as a witness to His salvation and His presence in and among them. And the always-faithful God gave them everything they needed to pass His test.

You can pass God's test, but it's not a "gimmy." Earlier, I said that you can be weakened by your trials—significantly—even fatally. Later in his letter, James will say, *"You do not have, because you do not ask. You ask and do not receive, because you ask wrongly...."*[172]

If you seek God in your trials—count on God—ask God for what you need to endure and overcome them—He will make you steadfast in your faith. If you do not do as James (and Jesus before him) advised, the opposite will be true. Every hardship you experience without God will weaken you and whatever faith you had to begin with.

But it need not be so. You can pass God's test, every time. Ask God in faith for what you need and receive the steadfastness that will sustain you, come what may. Call upon God, whatever the hardship, and *"count it all joy,"* because you know what God will do.

---

[172] James 4:2-3, RSV.

Galatians 5:13-25 ESV

[13] For you were called to freedom, brothers. Only do not use your freedom as an opportunity for the flesh, but through love serve one another. [14] For the whole law is fulfilled in one word: "You shall love your neighbor as yourself." [15] But if you bite and devour one another, watch out that you are not consumed by one another.

[16] But I say, walk by the Spirit, and you will not gratify the desires of the flesh. [17] For the desires of the flesh are against the Spirit, and the desires of the Spirit are against the flesh, for these are opposed to each other, to keep you from doing the things you want to do. [18] But if you are led by the Spirit, you are not under the law. [19] Now the works of the flesh are evident: sexual immorality, impurity, sensuality, [20] idolatry, sorcery, enmity, strife, jealousy, fits of anger, rivalries, dissensions, divisions, [21] envy, drunkenness, orgies, and things like these. I warn you, as I warned you before, that those who do such things will not inherit the kingdom of God. [22] But the fruit of the Spirit is love, joy, peace, patience, kindness, goodness, faithfulness, [23] gentleness, self-control; against such things there is no law. [24] And those who belong to Christ Jesus have crucified the flesh with its passions and desires.

[25] If we live by the Spirit, let us also keep in step with the Spirit. [26] Let us not become conceited, provoking one another, envying one another.

Free to Bear Good Fruit

Matthew 7:15-20 ESV

[Jesus said:]

¹⁵ *"Beware of false prophets, who come to you in sheep's clothing but inwardly are ravenous wolves. ¹⁶ You will recognize them by their fruits. Are grapes gathered from thornbushes, or figs from thistles? ¹⁷ So, every healthy tree bears good fruit, but the diseased tree bears bad fruit. ¹⁸ A healthy tree cannot bear bad fruit, nor can a diseased tree bear good fruit. ¹⁹ Every tree that does not bear good fruit is cut down and thrown into the fire. ²⁰ Thus you will recognize them by their fruits."*

10.

Free to Bear Good Fruit

Galatians 5:13-25; Matthew 7:15-20 ESV

Go into a grocery store, and the first place you come to is probably "the Produce Section." The first thing you're likely to see is fruit—apples and oranges, bananas and grapes—lemons, limes, peaches and pears. If they do their job right, the produce managers will almost overwhelm you with their wonderful array of fruit—fresh fruit—good fruit—desirable fruit.

Good fruit *is* desirable—because it is good. And knowing that, the folks who put the produce out are quick to take the bad fruit away, or at least hide it out of sight at the bottom of the pile. People are looking for good fruit.

Of course, good fruit doesn't show up in the grocery store by accident. People from all over work hard to harvest good fruit, package it and transport it to the store. Before that, they tend the trees upon which the fruit will grow. Fruit trees produce fruit after their kind, and good trees produce good fruit. That's how it is—and how it's always been.[173]

And for that reason, both Jesus and the Apostle Paul use the image of fruit and the trees that produce fruit to talk about the

---

[173] Genesis 1:11-12.

Christian life. Jesus points out that the fruit growing from a tree will tell you what kind of tree it is: apples grow from apple trees—oranges from orange trees. Simple, but significant.

And Jesus also points out that the quality of the fruit that grows on a tree will reveal the condition of the tree: the fruit a healthy tree produces will have to be good fruit and cannot be bad fruit. Again, obviously true, and yet, deceptively profound.

In the end, Jesus is focused on the importance of the health of the tree and the kind of tree that is capable of producing good fruit.

༻༺

The Apostle Paul comes at the matter from a different direction. Paul points to the wonderful fruit produced by a particular kind of tree and contrasts this remarkable fruit with anything produced any other way.

And if the fruit tree is the image of mankind, its ability to produce good fruit is not something it can accomplish on its own.

Paul is not saying to people—to Christians: "Produce good fruit." He is not saying to you: "Be loving, joyful, at peace." He is not saying, "Be patient, kind, good, faithful, gentle, and self-controlled; or be these things more than you have been.

What he is saying is that you cannot *be* these things in and of yourself, no matter how hard you try.

Under normal conditions, you don't have it in you to produce that kind of fruit—good fruit. Under normal conditions, the fruit you can produce is so awful—so rotten—it isn't worth calling it "fruit."

Paul calls it "works"—*"works of the flesh"*—what results when you and everybody else in the world do exactly what you—we—feel like doing. His offhand list is long and ugly and is a pretty fair summary of the world we live in today and watch on TV every night—underwritten by corporate sponsors eager to advertise on the coattails of the moral corruption played out in shameless detail before our increasingly jaded eyes. It makes sense that, in an anything-goes world, "everything-that-comes" will not be the best of what's possible, but the worst.

But here's the surprise: the rules, regulations and restrictions of religious legalism don't produce good fruit, either. There is no more love, joy, peace or any of the other stuff Paul listed as fruits of the Spirit, in servitude to all the Laws in the Old Testament than there is in wild and total rebellion against them. Neither Law nor license produces good fruit...

...which is why Paul is a fanatic about the freedom from the Law Christ's death made possible. *"For you were called to freedom, brothers...,"* he tells the Galatians. If he were emailing them, I suspect this part would be in all-caps and bold face type with an abundance of exclamation points.

"Called"—by Whom? *"...to freedom"*—from what?—and for what?

ಶ್ಞ

The Crucifixion of Jesus—and His ministry that preceded it—was God's call, to any who would believe in Jesus, to shed the shackles of their stifling, suffocating servitude to a system of rules that rendered a loving, living relationship between God and anyone beyond anyone's reach. Like He did with Lazarus, bound up and laid away in a grave to rot, Jesus comes and calls to everyone bound up in legalism, *"Come out!"*[174]

And just as Jesus commanded the people around Lazarus to remove what bound him and let him go free, so Paul had heard the Risen Christ command him to bring that same freedom to everyone Jesus called.[175] And despite the opposition he ran into everywhere, Paul proclaimed that freedom. He proclaimed freedom from the Law.[176]

---

[174] John 11:38-44.
[175] Acts 9:1-16.
[176] Romans 8:2.

Keeping the Law—to be of any value—had to be done perfectly—which it could not be.[177]

And if the Law could not be kept perfectly, keeping it imperfectly accomplished nothing in terms of overcoming the breach between you and God. That breach would be—and was—overcome only by God's act of grace in Jesus, as it never could be by any act of sinful man.[178]

Paul proclaimed freedom from the Law—but not freedom for lawlessness. Both the Law as an end in itself, and lawlessness—moral license—as a law unto itself, are forms of slavery rather than freedom.

But as soon as he used the word, Paul followed it up with an equally stern warning: *"...do not use your freedom as an opportunity for the flesh...."*

How easy it is to hear "Freedom!" and think, "Anything goes!"

But you know better.

☙❧

The freedom Jesus gives to all who answer His call is not a freedom "to do whatever you *want*." It is the freedom, finally, "to be able to do what you *should*." It is the freedom to let God do what you cannot do—to let God grow His holy fruit in you.

When Paul lays out a list of virtues to contrast the vices he stacked up on the "rap sheet" of the world, he isn't telling you to behave better. Of course, he's certainly not telling you to cut loose and behave badly, either.

What he is saying is that the characteristics of godly virtue can blossom in your life—not because you have the ability to bring them forth—but because God's Spirit can grow this kind of "fruit" in you. And will.

---

[177] James 2:10.
[178] Ephesians 2:8.

And that is because before the fruit of the Spirit becomes the glorious evidence of the Holy Spirit's presence and activity in you, it is, and has always been, the fruit—*of* the *Spirit.*

Love, joy, peace, patience, kindness, goodness, faithfulness, gentleness, and self-control are aspects of God Himself, as Father, Son and Holy Spirit. They are aspects—though not the only ones—that operate eternally within the very nature of our God. And the evidence of these fruits of the Sprit reveals things about this God to us that suggest what He is doing in His interaction with us—and the traits that He desires to develop in us as part of the redeemed and sanctified nature into which He desires to transform us.

࿐

We've been talking about the fruit of the Spirit, but Paul mentions the Spirit a half-dozen times in these few verses in Galatians—and each time, in a slightly different way. He talks about the fruit of the Spirit—and the desires of the Spirit. He says, *"the desires of the Spirit are against the flesh"*—the physical, self-centered, sinful and all-too-human urges that rule so much of our lives and our world. That makes sense.

But have you ever considered that the Holy Spirit—God—has desires—things that God wants—and, presumably, exerts Himself to obtain?

Certainly, the desires of the Spirit are against the desires of the flesh—so that when you are tempted by the ways of the flesh, you're not the only one wanting you to overcome that temptation. The Holy Spirit desires that victory for you as well. Bearing the fruit of the Spirit requires walking by the Spirit, which means being led by the Spirit, which results in your keeping in step with the Spirit as you live by the Spirit.

You don't produce the fruit of the Spirit; the Spirit produces it in you. Choosing to move through life—to confront the challenges of each day—in harmony and companionship with the Holy Spirit

Free to Bear Good Fruit

is to walk by the Spirit—to desire what the Spirit desires. The Spirit does not desire to follow you—especially if where you choose to go is after the desires of the flesh that seduce you into thoughts and deeds unworthy of the Spirit.

The Holy Spirit desires to lead you so that wherever you go you will find yourself in the kind of moral and spiritual climate where you can bear the fruit of the Spirit. And when you walk with the Spirit so faithfully that He is always leading you, you eventually find yourself, not just walking with the Spirit, but walking *in step* with the Spirit, stepping where He has stepped, even as a soldier might walk safely through a minefield by putting his feet where his leader put his and so marked the way.[179]

The way of the flesh is a minefield, full of danger for the wayward soul. One false step—one poor choice—one wrong move—and all the promise and possibility of life can be blown away in an instant.

But the promise and great possibilities of life are safe and secure when you walk by the Spirit and live by the Spirit.

After you are freed from the Law, there are two ways in life—the way of the flesh and the way of the Spirit. Life in the Spirit bears good fruit. What life in the flesh bears is all too clear and not worth mentioning.

You are free to choose the way you will go. Christ set you free from Law and lawlessness. Follow the Spirit and, *with* the Spirit, bear much fruit.

---

[179] This image was suggested by the story of General Norman Schwarzkopf's efforts as a battalion commander in Vietnam, intentionally entering a minefield in an attempt to rescue several soldiers trapped there.

Hebrews 12:5-11 ESV

The Book of Hebrews was written at a time when Christians were facing growing hostility from the world. The writer points to a father's responsibility to mold and shape the character and faith of his children as an example of what God is doing in the lives of Christians as we endure the opposition of our culture.

⁵ And have you forgotten the exhortation that addresses you as sons?
  "My son, do not regard lightly
    the discipline of the Lord,
    nor be weary when reproved by him.
  ⁶ For the Lord disciplines the one he loves,
    and chastises every son whom he receives."
⁷ It is for discipline that you have to endure. God is treating you as sons. For what son is there whom his father does not discipline? ⁸ If you are left without discipline, in which all have participated, then you are illegitimate children and not sons. ⁹ Besides this, we have had earthly fathers who disciplined us and we respected them. Shall we not much more be subject to the Father of spirits and live? ¹⁰ For they disciplined us for a short time as it seemed best to them, but he disciplines us for our good, that we may share his holiness. ¹¹ For the moment all discipline seems painful rather than pleasant, but later it yields the peaceful fruit of righteousness to those who have been trained by it.

Build Your House
Matthew 7:24-27 ESV

Jesus concludes the Sermon on the Mount with a comparison of the results of building on solid versus shifting foundations. The lesson applies to building physical houses, and to building faith and families as well.

[Jesus said:]
²⁴ "Everyone then who hears these words of mine and does them will be like a wise man who built his house on the rock. ²⁵ And the rain fell, and the floods came, and the winds blew and beat on that house, but it did not fall, because it had been founded on the rock. ²⁶ And everyone who hears these words of mine and does not do them will be like a foolish man who built his house on the sand. ²⁷ And the rain fell, and the floods came, and the winds blew and beat against that house, and it fell, and great was the fall of it."

11.

Build Your House

Hebrews 12:5-11; Matthew 7:24-27 ESV

The fabric of society is fraying. Our culture is coming apart. And when, in the decades to come, scavengers rummage among the ruins of what "used to be," and wonder why it all came crashing down, they may not realize that the answer was as simple as this: fathers did not bother to "build their houses." Or if they did—when they did—they built on sand rather than rock.

You can see the advancing images of this terrifying future in the news reports and entertainment offerings of our day: the acceptance and legalization of mood- and mind-altering drug use; the rising frequency and ferocity of violence by organized gangs and random individuals; the acceptance and celebration of immorality disguised as a brave and noble commitment to equality and tolerance; the intensifying hostility to Christianity and growing efforts on many fronts to curtail its activities and influence; the widespread neglect and rejection of marriage as the gateway to sexual activity and the proper environment for children to be conceived and nurtured.

But behind all this is a pattern of fathers not building their houses—their families—on solid rock.

It is not my intention or desire to beat up on the fathers who are here today. On Mothers' Day, moms get heaps of praise and gratitude. On Fathers' Day, dads should not get dumped on.

But let me put the challenge you're facing as fathers—Christian fathers—in perspective and help you equip yourself for your God-given responsibility and privilege. And even more importantly, let me talk to mothers and fathers—and grandparents, aunts and uncles—of boys who will grow into men—*if* they are raised with a discerning appreciation of what they are being raised for—*if* they are led to see the godly purpose of their manhood, which is your responsibility.

All across our country, for a generation and more, boys have been allowed to grow up physically without being formed into men—without being disciplined, trained and required—forced, where necessary—to become men at the end of their adolescence. Our society has encouraged the extension of childhood beyond high school, beyond college, beyond the decade of the 20s.

And so, a multitude of male human beings—old enough to be men, but allowed to remain boys, emotionally, psychologically, and morally—have undermined the foundation of our society by omission and commission—by failing to be and act like men—by remaining boys, and acting like it. In our permissive society, where technology has reduced the natural consequences of immoral acts, and secularism has removed their stigma, boys in their teens and 20s and 30s feel free to enjoy the pleasures of manhood without accepting the responsibilities that men should shoulder. And as any immature child will do, they take what is at hand with no thought for the consequences, to themselves or others.

And they have been abetted in their immaturity and immorality by parents who are too much focused on meeting material needs and too much afraid to oppose the rising tide of immorality around them. The perpetual male adolescent has been abetted in his moral irresponsibility by foolish girls who value attention and popularity more than their virtue and the better future they have been deceived into throwing away. And worst of all, the abettors are the leaders of institutions who create the environments of immorality that boys and men-who-will-not-grow-up exist in and adapt their perspectives and behaviors to.

And so there is in our country a growing epidemic of children conceived by fathers who have no ability and no desire to fulfill their paternal responsibilities. There is a growing epidemic of men who will not marry the women who bear their children or will not remain faithful to them if they do marry them at some point. There is a growing epidemic of men—including men in the military and on college campuses—assaulting girls and women who will not consent to their sexual advances—or perhaps assaulting them because consent has become so commonplace that it is insufficiently stimulating for those whose only goal in life is to see how much they can get away with.

And, as a result, more and more families are built without fathers—or with the poorest excuses for fathers—by women who are financially handicapped and emotionally wounded, for children who were the product, not of selfless love and lifelong commitment, but of immaturity, irresponsibility and indifference to the innocent and helpless lives that would result from irresponsible behavior.

And more and more children are growing up in homes without the sacrificial example and positive moral discipline of strong godly fathers. A generation of immature men and women has grown up—or not grown up—using each other to satisfy selfish interests and receiving no genuine affirmation in the process. Violence increases and trust decreases across our country. Everyone, victim and victimizer alike, ends up alone. And society unravels like a fabric from which individual threads are pulled away…

…which is why things must change—why fathers must build their houses—their families—and build them on the solid rock of

Jesus. Our society's future will be determined by the future of our families and the future of our families will be determined by the moral and spiritual foundations of the men who are and will become our families' fathers. It is as simple and significant as that.

And Jesus said, *"Everyone who hears these words of mine and puts them into practice is like a wise man who built his house on the rock."*

Fathers—and fathers to be: your families, now and for generations to come, will be made strong and successful more by your hearing and practicing what Jesus has said than anything else. The happiness of your wives and the wellbeing of your children, and of their children, and of their children's children when you are long in your grave, will be determined by how well you build your own spiritual foundation on Jesus, first—and then by how well you establish your marriage and your family on that same foundation in the time God allots to you.

When Jesus used this example of building a house, He was talking about a physical structure. But in the Bible, a man's house has often meant his family, those living under his roof and those who will be his descendants forever after him. God told King David, "You will not build Me a house, but I will build you a house—*I will raise up your offspring to succeed you, your own flesh and blood....*"[180] And so God did, till the House of David produced the Savior of the world.

The Psalmist wrote, *"Unless the LORD builds the house, the builders labor in vain,"*[181] which seems to imply that without God help, a father cannot build his house successfully—cannot put the proper foundation under his marriage or his family. Without God's help and guidance, a father's best intentions will fail. "All other ground," as the hymn says, "is sinking sand."[182]

---

[180] 2 Samuel 7:12, NIV.
[181] Psalm 127:1, NIV.
[182] From Edward Mote, "My Hope is Built on Nothing Less," 1834.

From Matthew 7

C. S. Lewis once wrote, "There are lots of nice things you can do with sand: but do not try building a house on it."[183] And Jesus said it was the foolish man who built his house on the sand, because that house and every house is going to be hit by the powerful storms of life. The house on the rock stands, but the house on sand is blown away.

And so, I repeat: "All other ground is sinking sand."

Build your house on the Rock. Anchor your life—anchor your marriage—anchor your children, sons and daughters alike—on the Rock Who enables you—and them—to withstand every storm.

"But I'm not really that religious."

Then *get* religious—for the sake of your house, your family, your future. Get some solid rock under you for a change, and the sooner the better.

In other words, let Jesus make God your Father; let Jesus make *you* God's son. And then make your Heavenly Father your model for fatherhood. Let Jesus help you grow up into spiritual maturity as a man of God—whatever your age.

❧

So how will you build your house, now that you are a father—or when you become a father? The secret is divinely inspired discipline.

The reading in Hebrews says, *"Endure hardship as discipline."* For the sake of your children, accept the hardships you encounter with manly maturity. God corrects us when we do wrong—for our benefit. And even when we do right, God uses the difficulties we experience in life through no fault of our own to form us and strengthen us and make us better men.

Do the same with your sons and daughters. Do not be afraid to correct what is wrong, and do not be too quick to remove all difficulty from their path, for you will not always be there to do so.

---

[183] C. S. Lewis, *The Complete C. S. Lewis Signature Classics,* Grand Rapids, MI: Zondervan, 2007, p. 154.

And the strength and wisdom gained in facing hardships and disappointments in childhood build character and maturity for adulthood later on.

The mission of every boy is to become a godly man so that, if it is God's will, he is ready and able to build his own house—his own family—under the Fatherhood of God. Make sure that your sons know that, and that nothing in their experience of childhood prevents them or delays them from progressing toward manhood and maturity in their proper time.

Teach your sons that the daughters of other fathers are to be respected as the partners they will become for some man in the future. Girls and women are not to be treated as objects of conquest to be collected and discarded as opportunity allows. Teach your son that some father's daughter will grow up to be *his* wife and partner for life—the woman who will bear the children God chooses to give him—and that he must devote himself to becoming the man who is worthy of such a priceless gift. Discipline your sons if you would be a wise and godly father.

And if you are a father of daughters, discipline them as well. Show them the respect and selfless love they should expect and demand from every boy and man they encounter as they grow up. Treat their mothers with that same respect and love. Do not let your daughters define themselves, at any age, in attitude, actions or appearance, as less than what God has created them to be. Show them what a man who has built his house on the solid Rock looks like and lives like—and how they may depend on him.

Some of you fathers are doing these things already. I have seen you. You have placed your life and your marriage and your family on the strong and safe foundation. You are building your house on the Rock. Your sons are becoming men, and your daughters are becoming women who will be worthy of godly men.

But there are too many foolish men—and too many boys who should be men—building too many houses on sand. We need

From Matthew 7

more men—more fathers—to build their houses on the solid Rock.

Pray that God will turn our nation's boys into men and our men into wise and godly fathers, for the sake of their children—and the society that cannot survive otherwise.

From Matthew 8

Isaiah 43:1-7 ESV

¹ *But now thus says the* LORD,
 he who created you, O Jacob,
 he who formed you, O Israel:
"Fear not, for I have redeemed you;
 I have called you by name, you are mine.
² *When you pass through the waters,*
 I will be with you;
 and through the rivers,
 they shall not overwhelm you;
when you walk through fire
 you shall not be burned,
 and the flame
 shall not consume you.
³ *For I am the* LORD *your God,*
 the Holy One of Israel, your Savior.
I give Egypt as your ransom,
 Cush and Seba in exchange for you.
⁴ *Because you are precious in my eyes,*
 and honored, and I love you,
I give men in return for you,
 peoples in exchange for your life.
⁵ *Fear not, for I am with you;*
 I will bring your offspring from the east,
 and from the west I will gather you.
⁶ *I will say to the north, Give up,*
 and to the south, Do not withhold;
 bring my sons from afar
 and my daughters from the end of the earth,
⁷ *everyone who is called by my name,*
 whom I created for my glory,
 whom I formed and made."

ঔ

Just Passing Through

Matthew 8:23-27 ESV

²³ And when [Jesus] got into the boat, his disciples followed him. ²⁴ And behold, there arose a great storm on the sea, so that the boat was being swamped by the waves; but he was asleep. ²⁵ And they went and woke him, saying, "Save us, Lord; we are perishing." ²⁶ And he said to them, "Why are you afraid, O you of little faith?" Then he rose and rebuked the winds and the sea, and there was a great calm. ²⁷ And the men marveled, saying, "What sort of man is this, that even winds and sea obey him?"

12.

Just Passing Through

Isaiah 43:1-7; Matthew 8:23-27 ESV

I remember a time when parents—loving, caring, committed parents—spanked their children when their children were disobedient, disrespectful or rebellious. Loving and caring mothers and fathers inflicted punishment—pain—on their own flesh and blood to disciple them and deter them from behaviors and attitudes that, if left unchecked, would bring the children harsher punishments and greater pain later in their lives, inflicted, this time, by a callous and uncaring world.

If a beloved child would not "learn his lesson" in those long-ago days, a parent might be forced, eventually, to impose a greater punishment: withholding parental protection and letting the foolish child do whatever he wished—and suffer the consequences that naturally came with doing what had been expressly and repeatedly forbidden.

Either way, these loving parents did not stop loving their children when they punished them. They grieved the necessity of doing so—and the suffering their children's determined disobedience brought upon them.

And so it was with God's children—first the northern kingdom of Israel and then Judah in the south. They disobeyed their Heavenly Father, again and again. Generation after generation, they rebelled against His loving, caring discipline. And God punished His wayward children, imposing plagues and withholding rain, and sending foreign armies to devour their land like locust. And, at last, this Heavenly Father just let His beloved, bull-headed children have their way—and the catastrophic consequences that came with it: defeat, destruction and exile—just like God's prophets predicted.

~·~

It's a story most people no longer read. They don't know what happened and so miss the point as it applies today. The point is that what happened once can happen again. When I forgot what I got spanked for, I often got spanked again. Rebellious children in every generation remain at risk of the discipline of their devoted parents—whether human or heavenly.

We look at the crumbling moral and spiritual foundation of our culture, brought about by widespread acts of disobedience and flagrant attitudes of rebellion, and we sense the judgment that God can impose upon our people—the judgment He has imposed on others in the past—on people that He dearly loved. What society cannot see—and will not hear—we see and hear because we look to our God and listen. And we are frightened at the prospect of divine punishment, whether actively inflicted or passively allowed. Is that what we are experiencing—in America and the world today? Is that all we have to look forward to in the future that lies before us?

After a lifetime in exile, the people heard from the God Who sent them there to punish them. Yes, they got what they deserved. Yes, it was their own fault. "But now," Isaiah tells them, "your Heavenly Father has something to say."

"You may be in exile—you may be in a bad place—but you need to know that, because you are Mine, you are 'just passing through.' Your 'home' is somewhere else. Your home is with Me. And I am going to bring you home."

Listen to what God is telling the exiles—people who have spent a lifetime lost and languishing in a seemingly hopeless place: "Do not be afraid! Do not be afraid because I have redeemed you. I have paid the debt you could not pay yourself. I have gone your bail. I am ripping the door off the dungeon where you have been rotting away and I am taking you away from all this."

Listen to how personal this is: *"I have called you by name,"* says God. *"You are Mine."*

Listen to how powerful this is: *"I am the Lord your God,* [I am] *...your Savior.* I will not let floods overwhelm you. I will not let fires consume you. I give whole countries in exchange for you! Wherever you are—wherever in the whole wide world—I will bring you home."

That's a "no child left behind" promise of divine proportions!

And listen to how intimately loving this is: *"You are precious in My eyes.* You are priceless to Me. *I love you."* This is the word Isaiah brings from God to the Jews, captives sitting around their compound in the suburbs of someone else's capital city.[184]

But God says He's gathering all His children from all corners of the globe—from the ends of the earth. So God has plans for every one of His children who has gone astray and away from His parental love and protection. Their Father had a purpose for punishing them—and He has a purpose for going and getting them.

After all, a loving parent never gives up on a rebellious child, no matter how often that son or daughter breaks the parent's heart.[185] That's not the way that kind of love works.

❧

---

[184] Isaiah 43:14.
[185] Hosea 11:1-9.

All this is Old Testament prophecy—the promise of salvation for people who don't have a prayer—hope in the midst of hard times and unhappy circumstances.

So, can we get in on this good news, or does this message belong in a museum?

Well, if our Heavenly Father still loves us enough to discipline us—to let us suffer the consequences of our disobedience, waywardness and sin—maybe He will still do the loving thing and lift us up when we have learned our lesson. Maybe the God Who created and formed us—just like He did the children of Israel of old—will still redeem us and claim us and call us by name. When we pass through the stormy waters of life, will He be with us, too?

Funny you should ask.

❧

There was a time, centuries after Isaiah, when some of the descendants of those same exiles were stuck in a significant storm of their own. Little boat. Large problem. It looked to them as though Judgment Day was minutes away.

And then they discovered that they had a Savior, too. They were being swamped, and the One Who could keep them afloat was sleeping through the storm in the bow of the boat. They called out in their fear and Jesus showed them why their fear was misplaced.

He rose up from his sleep in the boat—as He would later rise up from His sleep in the tomb. He took control of the winds and the waves as He would one day take control of Death itself—to give the kind of life that even Death cannot diminish.

They were His disciples. They were supposed to be learning discipline from Him: right behavior and right attitudes. What they learned that day was that winds and waves obeyed divine directives better than they did.

What Jesus was saying to them was the same thing God was saying to His "exiled-for-a-reason" children: "Don't you realize that living your life as though this world is all there is is always going to backfire on you? I'm not going to let you get away with living a life of disobedience and rebellion here—because you're 'just passing through.'"

A good parent disciplines a child so that the child will not suffer more as life goes on and the stakes and opportunities for self-inflicted wounds grow greater. God disciplines His children in the same way and for the same purpose—and for more. Spiritually, we are God's children, growing up in His family to live here—and for eternity—in loving submission and celebration.

We are on our way home with our Heavenly Father. We have some wicked waters to pass through—and the waves would overwhelm us, if our Father and His Son and His Holy Spirit were not with us. This life is aflame with fiery trials that we must face—but we can endure them all with God's help. And if we do, we need never fear the "forever fire" that awaits those who are unwilling to understand why we must conform to our Father's will.[186]

Hear this—when all you can see are the towering waves crashing down upon you, and all you can feel is the horrifying heat raging all around you: "Do not be afraid, for I have already taken care of your survival. I have not forgotten you. I have not lost track of you. I know you by name and I am with you. I will always be with you. I will always calm the waves and quench the flames. I would give—and have given—whatever it takes to save you. You are My infinitely and eternally beloved child."

❧

You and I are just "passing through" this life. It's a hard life because so many people messed up so many things for so long before us. And we add our share as we go along, like foolish, mischievous children who can't leave well enough alone.

---

[186] Matthew 25:31-46.

Just Passing Through

Whatever we are going through—sickness, sorrow, guilt or shame, danger, conflict, fear or want—we are going *through* it. It is not permanent—however long it lasts in this life. The God Who loves us and is with us will not leave us there forever. He will redeem it—or deliver us from it—in *this* world—or in the next. However low we go, our loving Father will raise us up, if we let Him.[187] However far away we roam from His love and leadership, He will come for us and carry us to the place He has prepared for us.[188]

❧⋅❧

When Jesus calmed the winds and the waves, men who thought they knew Him could only wonder: "What kind of Man *is* this?!"

They would learn in time.

And when God spoke up and told the exiles, "Let's go home!"—and then they did—they had to wonder: "What kind of *God* is this?!"—even though He had been their God for a thousand years.

❧⋅❧

Frankly, the future doesn't look so good. We may be facing a perfect storm of the imposition of our Heavenly Father's discipline as the world rises up in ever more egregious rebellion against His divine authority. We have every reason to be afraid of what awaits us in the days to come—except that the Holy One of Israel says, "Don't be, for I am with you. Don't be afraid, for I have redeemed you." And the Stiller of storms says, "Why are you afraid? I will get you through what you think will do you in."

Water and fire. Waves and flames. That's what life is like because we've made it so. But we who are called by God's Name

---

[187] Romans 8:11.
[188] John 14:2-3; 1 Thessalonians 4:16-17.

From Matthew 8

have His promise: We will pass through the waters and not be overwhelmed. We will walk through the fire and not be consumed by it.

Our Father is taking us home, just like He promised—through it all.

Look Who's Invited to Dinner

Matthew 9:9-13 NRSV

⁹ As Jesus was walking along, he saw a man called Matthew sitting at the tax booth; and he said to him, "Follow me." And he got up and followed him.

¹⁰ And as he sat at dinner in the house, many tax collectors and sinners came and were sitting with him and his disciples. ¹¹ When the Pharisees saw this, they said to his disciples, "Why does your teacher eat with tax collectors and sinners?" ¹² But when he heard this, he said, "Those who are well have no need of a physician, but those who are sick. ¹³ Go and learn what this means, 'I desire mercy, not sacrifice.' For I have come to call not the righteous but sinners."

13.

Look Who's Invited to Dinner

Matthew 9:9-13 NRSV

We are apparently to understand the reading in Matthew today as the story of Matthew's call as a disciple. Jesus comes along—without an appointment—and says *"Follow Me,"* which is one of those phrases like, "We found a little something on your x-rays," that really means a lot more than it says.

Jesus is giving Matthew an opportunity to trade everything for the chance to become part of the inner circle of Jesus. And, according to the Bible, Matthew drops everything—which is quite a lot (like his career and his enviable standard of living)—and takes off with Jesus.

Now Matthew isn't a particularly religious fellow—he collects taxes for a foreign government—or one of their greedy puppet kings. And so, as you might expect, his friends aren't particularly religious, either. But when Jesus calls him and he follows, one of the first things Matthew does is to invite his friends—such as they are—to meet Jesus.

Matthew thinks his friends should meet Jesus—probably thinks they would want to. Now, is that because they "need" Jesus (which they certainly do), or because Matthew knows that his friends, the other tax collectors and various individuals officially designated by the religious establishment as "sinners," will really like Jesus and enjoy Him—if they get the chance to meet Him?

And now that Matthew has answered the call of Jesus to follow Him and become a disciple, Matthew has the opportunity, for the first time, to introduce his friends to this remarkable Jesus. As you know, it's rather awkward, and sometimes virtually impossible, to introduce people to someone you *don't* know.

So Matthew introduces his friends to Jesus. And interestingly enough, Jesus wants to meet them and get to know them, despite their tarnished reputations, which, in most cases, are well deserved.

Isn't it amazing who Jesus wants to spend His time with? Isn't it amazing who gathers around Him at the table? And He lets them! He invites them and welcomes them with honor—tax collectors and *sinners!*—despite the well-known, dishonorable lives they have been—and may still be—living.

If you were putting the guest list together for a dinner party with Jesus, who would you instinctively put on the list? Who would you intentionally leave off?

And the more important question: How different would your list be from the one Jesus would put together Himself—and why? How likely would you be to be included on His list—and how comfortable would you be, if you were on the list, with the other people at the party?

The answers to these questions have a lot to do with the purpose of a "Jesus banquet." When Jesus sits down with people, it is not to honor them or entertain them. Jesus shares a meal with a person to feed the person. The people Jesus invites to share a meal—and the people Jesus encourages His disciples to invite—are *hungry* people. Otherwise, they would not come.

Now, here's the shame of it: Some people get so busy with business or their hobbies that they don't realize they're hungry. It's happened to me from time to time. I'm told it's not good for you; it's not conducive to good, long-term health. When you're hungry—when you need nourishment—you ought to come and eat.

But don't look too carefully at who else is gathered around the table if you're squeamish about who you share your meals with. There is no "moral dress code" here, except for faith in His forgiveness and grace. There's no executive dining room in the Kingdom of God—or in the Church His Son, Jesus Christ, founded.

Everybody gathers to be fed. The good news is: There's always a place for you—and for whomever you decide to bring with you. Jesus was always feeding somebody. Sometimes, He fed thousands all at once.[189] Sometimes, He fed one man or one woman at a time.[190]

But however many (or few) dinner guests He had, Jesus always made sure every one was fully fed—completely satisfied. No one who ever came to Jesus ever went away hungry, except by his own choosing.

Jesus is always able to satisfy the hunger and quench the thirst you bring to Him. He is always able to feed you and fill you with all good things.

&-&

Groucho Marx used to say, "I would never consider joining an organization that would let someone like me become a member."[191]

---

[189] John 6:1-13; Matthew 15:38.
[190] John 4:3-26; John 3:1-21.
[191] Groucho Marx, *Groucho and Me: The Autobiography*, New York, NY: Da Capo Press, 2009, p. 321.

On the other hand, Roger Munger has said, "The Church is the only fellowship in the world where the one requirement for membership is the absolute unworthiness of the candidate."[192]

So today, like every day, Jesus is calling disciples, unworthy as they are: *"Come, follow me."* [193] And today, as most days, His disciples end up at His table to be fed, not because they *deserve* to be there, but because they *need* to be there—to receive what Jesus has and wants to give.

Jesus extends the call of discipleship, the invitation to dine with Him, to all. The southern version goes "Come and get it."

Oh, and bring your friends. They're going to love this Guy, Jesus. And He loves them already.

---

[192] Robert Munger (d. 2001), Professor of Evangelism at Fuller Theological Seminary, quoted in Charles H. Talbert, *Reading Luke: A Literary and Theological Commentary*, London: Smyth & Helwys Publishers, Inc., p. 64.
[193] Luke 18:22, RSV.

Matthew 9:37-38; 10:1-8, 16 ESV

9 *³⁷ Then [Jesus] said to his disciples, "The harvest is plentiful, but the laborers are few; ³⁸ therefore ask the Lord of the harvest to send out laborers into his harvest."*

10 *¹ Then Jesus summoned his twelve disciples and gave them authority over unclean spirits, to cast them out, and to cure every disease and every sickness. ² These are the names of the twelve apostles: first, Simon, also known as Peter, and his brother Andrew; James son of Zebedee, and his brother John; ³ Philip and Bartholomew; Thomas and Matthew the tax collector; James son of Alphaeus, and Thaddaeus; ⁴ Simon the Cananaean, and Judas Iscariot, the one who betrayed him.*

⁵ These twelve Jesus sent out with the following instructions: "Go nowhere among the Gentiles, and enter no town of the Samaritans, ⁶ but go rather to the lost sheep of the house of Israel. ⁷ As you go, proclaim the good news, 'The kingdom of heaven has come near.' ⁸ Cure the sick, raise the dead, cleanse the lepers, cast out demons. You received without payment; give without payment."

¹⁶ "See, I am sending you out like sheep into the midst of wolves; so be wise as serpents and innocent as doves."

14.

Divine Assignment

Matthew 9:37-38; 10:1-8, 16 ESV

What do you see when you drive around town—when you go to the store or out to dinner—when you walk around your neighborhood or the golf course? What do you see in the people you encounter in the course of your day every day?

Everywhere Jesus went, He saw the potential for a great harvest of souls, and the need for helpers to join Him in the business of gathering people into the kingdom of God. Day after day, Jesus preached the gospel of salvation with unequalled authority.[194] Day after day, He performed miracles with supernatural power.[195] And then one day, Jesus gathered 12 men around Him, and said, "Now it's your turn."

These men were following Jesus because He was fascinating. Nobody ever did what He did. Nobody ever said the things He said—or said them the *way* He did. You've heard of "Must See TV"[196]? He was "Must see JC!"

---

[194] Matthew 7:28-29.
[195] Luke 4:36; 5:17.
[196] An advertising slogan used by NBC in the 1990s, and informally by many other people since.

Divine Assignment

Maybe Jesus was the One they had all been waiting for all their lives—the One the prophets had said would come one day. Maybe Jesus was "the Guy!" Wouldn't *that* be fascinating!

And, to tell the truth, whether He turned out to be the Messiah or not, they were also following Him because He was fun. Hang around Jesus and you got a taste of a better, more abundant life.[197] Jesus wasn't afraid of Pharisees or Sadducees[198]—or Roman soldiers, for that matter—all the people who terrified or annoyed them. Let the bad guys set a trap for Jesus and He would turn the tables on them with a simple question.[199] Let Him tell a story—and He would turn your whole understanding about life—and about God—upside down.[200]

Jesus made blind men see, deaf men hear, and cripples walk. Lepers were cleansed and lunatics came to their senses just because He said so.[201] Jesus could conjure up enough food to feed five thousand people—in the middle of nowhere, no less.[202] You never knew what He was going to do next—which is probably why these 12 disciples didn't see their divine assignment coming.

※

But *you* should. If you're following Jesus today for the fun or fascination of it, you best face up to the fact that He's got a divine assignment for you, too: "Take part in the harvest."

"There's a lot of harvesting to be done," Jesus says, *"but the workers are few."*

You see, Jesus didn't come to fascinate followers or make life fun. The miracles and the teaching were not the end, but the means to the end. Jesus came to conduct a harvest for the Lord of the Harvest—to gather people into the kingdom of heaven. But He

---

[197] John 10:10.
[198] Matthew 16:1-4.
[199] Matthew 21:23-27.
[200] Luke 10:25-37.
[201] Matthew 11:4-5; Luke 8:26-36.
[202] Mark 6:32-44.

does not intend to do all the work Himself, though there was *one* part that only He could do.

※

So, today, we review the receiving of our divine assignment. You did not receive your assignment today, unless you became a follower of Jesus for the first time today. You receive your assignment when you receive His salvation. When you have been harvested for the kingdom, you become a harvester with Jesus and the other disciples He has assigned to this, the ultimate work of God.

In a church where I once served, a life-long "church lady" told me one day—matter-of-factly and with no apparent embarrassment—that talking to people about Christianity was not the sort of thing she did.

I thought: Doesn't it concern you that you have refused to accept the assignment Jesus has given you? Do you even realize what you've done—to your relationship with Jesus—and to the fate of those who were *your* responsibility to harvest for the kingdom—by refusing the assignment?

I thought it—but I didn't say it.

But there *is* a divine harvest going on, and we have been assigned to participate in it. Still today, the harvest is plentiful. Hundreds of people come to this area every year, ready to be harvested for the kingdom of God. Thousands have been here for years, waiting to be harvested for the kingdom. You see them when you drive around town—when you go to the store or out to dinner—when you walk around your neighborhood or the golf course.

People will die an eternal death if they are not brought into the kingdom.[203] And churches will die, if these same people are not brought into the fellowship of a church.

---

[203] Matthew 13:40-43.

Divine Assignment

Jesus saw every person who was not following Him as a potential follower. And so should we. We should see every person who is not part of a local congregation as a potential member of our church. Every disciple has been assigned a role in the divine harvest Jesus has begun.

But how? How do you harvest effectively?

☙❧

It's all right there in the gospel we heard today. What did Jesus say?

First: *"Ask the Lord of the harvest…to send out workers into His harvest field."* Start with prayer. Ask the Lord for workers. Yes, you are one of them, but "many hands make light work" in physical assignments, and many hearts make inspired work in spiritual assignments.

Pray to the Lord of the harvest, because it is, after all, His harvest—His field—His crop of souls to be saved—not yours. You are not responsible for the result, but for the best effort you are able to provide. But prayer for the harvest strengthens your commitment to the work, which is part of the process for you.

☙❧

After telling His disciples to pray for the harvest, Jesus gave them divine authority, the same authority—the same power—His Heavenly Father gave Him to perform miracles. You are authorized and empowered to harvest for the kingdom. You are authorized and empowered to perform miracles of healing and overcoming evil to harvest effectively. Receive—accept—the power and authority to do things you know you cannot do without God's help. Jesus has given this power and authority to you.

Take it and use it to do your assignment…which requires that you go as directed. Jesus calls His followers together and empowers them, and then He sends them out. And where are you to go to harvest for God?

From Matthew 9 and 10

Jesus told the Twelve, "Don't go to places that are alien to you. Go to your own people. Go to those you know. Go to those who speak your language and share your world view."

So, start there. Surely you know someone who needs to be harvested for the kingdom of God. Surely you know someone who needs to be a part of this church. Start with those closest to you and easiest to talk to about their spiritual need. Later, you can branch out, or others can harvest other parts of the Lord's field who are more familiar with them.

Oh, and don't go harvesting alone. Did you notice, Matthew tells you who the Twelve were that Jesus sent to the harvest first? And he lists them in pairs: Peter and Andrew, James and John, all the way down to "Simon, the Zealot, and Judas Iscariot, who betrayed Him." The two sets of brothers, He sent out together. Friends, like Philip and Bartholomew, He made a team. Jesus did separate Matthew, the Roman collaborator, and Simon, the Zealot, who had sworn to kill all collaborators. But even Judas Iscariot was sent out to the harvest, partnered up, which sets the bar pretty low for the rest of us.

So who is your harvest partner—your teammate for your divine assignment? Is it a spouse or a sibling or a friend who is or will become closer than a brother? Is it a mentor who guides you or a novice who looks to you for help? Workers in the harvest work best together.

※

Jesus tells His disciples where to go and with whom. And He tells them—us—what to say in order to be effective in the work. "Proclaim this message," He said: *'The kingdom of heaven has come near.'"*

Keep it simple. Keep it personal. Keep it true: "This is what Jesus says. I believe it. It's working for me. I think it will work for you."

Divine Assignment

Whatever they're dealing with, that's the message. Whatever the question, that's the answer. Say what Jesus has told you to say...

...and do what He has enabled you to do.

"But I can't do miracles!"

Correct, only God can do miracles and, it just so happens, He has chosen to do them through you for those He wants you to harvest for the kingdom. You can't imagine what God can do through you if you show up and take part in the harvest. You don't know what word you say or deed you do or circumstance you set in motion will become, by God's grace, a miracle in the life of someone God sent you to harvest for Him.

Miracles are happening all the time. I'm not making this up; you are telling me so. The fact that some of you are here is a miracle in itself. And a lot of you are experiencing miracles because you *are* here, courtesy of God's harvest.

꽃

Whatever you say to people about Jesus—whatever you do through His power and under His authority—it is a gift that you are to give freely. We work in the harvest, giving freely to others, because God has given Jesus—and the kingdom—freely to us.

How do you harvest for the kingdom effectively?

Ask the Lord for more workers and receive the power and authority He gives you to participate in the harvest yourself. Go where God sends you, to those He would have you harvest, working with those spiritual partners He has provided to help and encourage you. Make your message the simple truth of the gospel and do not doubt that God has enabled you to work miracles in the lives of those you are to draw into the kingdom. Give freely since you have been given infinitely more than you could ever repay.

And be what your Lord has equipped you to be.

And what is that?

From Matthew 9 and 10

Jesus said, *"I am sending you out like sheep among wolves. Therefore, be as shrewd as snakes and as innocent as doves."*

The work of the harvest, by its very nature, leaves every worker vulnerable. You cannot do the work in safety, comfort, and convenience. Jesus took the ultimate risk for you. You will be subject to misunderstanding, rejection, hostility and stress for the sake of the work to which you are assigned. The work of the harvest can become costly to you, physically, emotionally, socially, and psychologically. But you are authorized the shield of divine shrewdness and the umbrella of holy innocence—and all for the sake of the harvest.

Can you be an effective worker in God's harvest? Can you harvest souls?

Pray, receive, go, speak, do, give, and be—as Jesus has assigned you—and you will see—not only what a miracle worker you will become in the Lord's field—but the wondrous harvest that God will accomplish through you for His kingdom.

Yes, our worship is wonderful, and our fellowship is fantastic, but there's harvesting to be done, too.

"And now," Jesus says, "it's your turn."

The Games of Childhood
Matthew 11:16-19, 25-30 NRSV

[Jesus said:]
¹⁶ "But to what will I compare this generation? It is like children sitting in the marketplaces and calling to one another,

> ¹⁷ *We played the flute for you,*
> *and you did not dance;*
> *we wailed,*
> *and you did not mourn.'*

¹⁸ "For John came neither eating nor drinking, and they say, 'He has a demon'; ¹⁹ the Son of Man came eating and drinking, and they say, 'Look, a glutton and a drunkard, a friend of tax collectors and sinners!' Yet wisdom is vindicated by her deeds."

²⁰ Then he began to reproach the cities in which most of his deeds of power had been done, because they did not repent. ²¹ "Woe to you, Chorazin! Woe to you, Bethsaida! For if the deeds of power done in you had been done in Tyre and Sidon, they would have repented long ago in sackcloth and ashes. ²² But I tell you, on the day of judgment it will be more tolerable for Tyre and Sidon than for you. ²³ And you, Capernaum, will you be exalted to heaven? No, you will be brought down to Hades.

"For if the deeds of power done in you had been done in Sodom, it would have remained until this day. ²⁴ But I tell you that on the day of judgment it will be more tolerable for the land of Sodom than for you."

²⁵ At that time Jesus said, "I thank you, Father, Lord of heaven and earth, because you have hidden these things from the wise and the intelligent and have revealed them to infants; ²⁶ yes, Father, for such was your gracious will. ²⁷ All things have been handed over to me by my Father; and no one knows the Son except the Father, and no one knows the Father except the Son and anyone to whom the Son chooses to reveal him.

²⁸ "Come to me, all you that are weary and are carrying heavy burdens, and I will give you rest. ²⁹ Take my yoke upon you, and learn from me; for I am gentle and humble in heart, and you will find rest for your souls. ³⁰ For my yoke is easy, and my burden is light."

15.

The Games of Childhood

Matthew 11:16-19, 25-30 NRSV

Vacation Bible School starts tomorrow here. There will be children everywhere doing all sorts of things. The children will learn a lot, but adults can learn a lot from them as well.

The same was true in the villages Jesus visited during His ministry. Children were everywhere doing all sorts of things. And Jesus made sure the grown-ups learned an important lesson from them.

Sometimes village children came to check Him out and He welcomed them, telling His disciples, *"Suffer the little children to come unto me, and forbid them not."*[204]

At other times, the village children were too busy playing their games to notice Him. But He noticed them. And He noticed a similarity between the games they were playing and His interaction with their parents and grandparents, the adults in the village.

Children love to play. Children love to use their imagination. They love to try things on: clothes, behaviors, attitudes. Jesus saw some children in a marketplace wanting to play "pretend."

---

[204] Mark 10:14, KJV.

The Games of Childhood

"Let's play 'wedding'—you dance." "Let's play 'funeral'—cry your eyes out." But these children weren't very happy. Things weren't going so well for these children Jesus saw in the village marketplace.

☙❧

Let's do a little review of child psychology: Children of a certain age are very concerned about the ground rules they play by. Break the rules and you mess up their game. Children of most every age want things to go their way. They want to play by their own rules. Some children are so concerned about their rules that they have a tendency to become bossy. And some children don't really want to play; they just want to sit on the sidelines where they can criticize and complain. These are not very attractive children—nor are the adults Jesus encountered who were acting just like them.

"Oh Jesus, play our favorite game and we'll love you. Dance to our music and You will be our friend. Work Yourself up over the causes on our agendas and You'll be okay in our book."

Remarkable how much the childish efforts to manipulate Jesus sound like the temptations He encountered in the wilderness at the beginning of His ministry: "If You will bow down and worship me...I will give You everything You want"[205]

But Jesus would not dance for the devil—or for the childish people sitting around in the places Jesus went, passing judgment on Him and His ministry.

Unlike people who act like bossy, self-absorbed children, Jesus is a grown-up—as John the Baptist was before Him. Sin is not a figment of imagination. Salvation is not a game.

God is revealing the kingdom of heaven to those who are willing to become "babes in Christ"—trusting, obedient children. But the whiney little brats who want everything—including Jesus

---

[205] Matthew 4:8-9.

From Matthew 11

and His salvation—*their* way, and *only* their way, are a different matter. God is concealed from the arrogant—the "know-it-alls"—and revealed to babes.

Beware, lest you become like the bossy children: "Lord, I'm active in church—I'm singing off Your sheet of music. Why aren't You curing my pain or keeping my kids out of trouble?"

"I'm putting my 'seat' in the pew and my check in the plate, why aren't you ending the war and fixing the economy?" After a while, you get to sounding like the grumpy little kids in the marketplace.

You cannot control God with tin whistles or temper tantrums. You cannot control Him with religious rites and sacred symbols, either. Call Him what you will—complain all you want about His non-compliance with your expectations and desires—and Jesus will not be phased at all, except to be amazed that people who should know better—people with a strong religious heritage—who read His Word and pray in His Name—continue to try to call the cadence for Jesus when salvation calls for commitment to *His* way—falling in line behind *Him*.

Paul wrote, *"When I was a child, I spoke like a child, I thought like a child, I reasoned like a child. When I became a man, I gave up childish ways."* [206]

"Oh Jesus, come and dance to our music."

And He says, "No, you come to Me. Put away your games of pretend and your other childish ways and take My yoke upon you. Stop complaining that I won't play your games and learn from Me what it means to be a grown-up saved by grace. Take My yoke upon you and you will discover what's better than all your games combined: *"...rest for your soul...."*

Jesus found that generation childish and churlish.

---

[206] 1 Corinthians 13:11, RSV.

The Games of Childhood

And what of this generation? What about us? Are you impatient with Jesus—or "in harness"—"yoked"—with Him? Are you offensive or obedient? Sulky or submissive?

Jesus says Wisdom is justified by her deeds. The wisest thing you can do these days is whatever He tells you to.

"Jesus, You won't play our games!"

No, but it would be wise to play His.

No kidding.

16.

Sowing Seeds—Bearing Fruit

Matthew 13:1-9 NRSV

¹ That same day Jesus went out of the house and sat beside the sea. ² Such great crowds gathered around him that he got into a boat and sat there, while the whole crowd stood on the beach. ³ And he told them many things in parables, saying: "Listen! A sower went out to sow. ⁴ And as he sowed, some seeds fell on the path, and the birds came and ate them up. ⁵ Other seeds fell on rocky ground, where they did not have much soil, and they sprang up quickly, since they had no depth of soil. ⁶ But when the sun rose, they were scorched; and since they had no root, they withered away. ⁷ Other seeds fell among thorns, and the thorns grew up and choked them. ⁸ Other seeds fell on good soil and brought forth grain, some a hundredfold, some sixty, some thirty. ⁹ Let anyone with ears listen!"

❦

A great symphony may not begin with a crash of cymbals or the piercing tones of the trumpet. A great work of art may forego dramatic colors for more subtle hues. And great truth may be expressed, not in spellbinding oratory, but in simple, everyday words. Jesus begins to share a significant spiritual truth in the 13th chapter of Matthew with a deceptively simple statement. He says, *"Listen, a sower went out to sow."*

Now, since you are listening to me and there is no "ticker" running across the bottom of the pulpit with words to read, I should probably clarify that the "sower" we're talking about is not the kind who works with needle and thread. This is not a tailor or seamstress, but a farm hand going out into a field to plant seeds, spelled: "s-O-w-e-r."

The sower went out to sow. That's what sowers do. A sower going out to sow is a common occurrence around the villages where Jesus spends His time.

Everybody listening to Jesus has seen a sower go out to sow. But no one who ever heard Jesus talk about it would ever see a sower the same way again

Jesus begins with the sower, but His focus is really on the process. This is "broadcast" seeding—the seed goes everywhere. The sower here sows by hand; you and I use those rolling spreaders with the little whirling trays underneath, but the result is pretty much the same: the seed goes everywhere.

Notice that Jesus talks a lot more about the seed than the sower. A seed may not seem like much, but it contains the power to bear fruit. Every seed this sower sows is good seed and has the potential to bear fruit.

Unfortunately, not all of it will. The nature or condition of the soil that receives the seed determines whether the seed that falls in that place will bear fruit.

Many who have heard this story over the centuries have asked, "Then why doesn't the sower till the soil before he sows the seed, or prepare it better, or make sure that he only drops the seed where the good soil is?"

The sower could certainly be more efficient and effective— from our modern perspective.

But the sower sows the seed everywhere because he wants it to bear fruit everywhere. How it is received has a lot to do with whether it will take root and bear fruit or not, but the seed is the essential element in the process. If the seed doesn't get there, it will

From Matthew 13

be impossible for the soil to bear fruit, no matter how fertile the soil is. Sowing is the essential first step in bearing fruit: no sowing—no scattering the seed—no fruit.

Now the sower knows exactly what seed he needs to sow in order to bear the fruit he wants. It would be a shame to go to all the trouble to sow seed if you're broadcasting the wrong seed or a defective version. The sower knows: Sow the seed, but make sure you're got the right stuff when you do.

The sower sows the right seed, and there is apparently enough seed to sow it everywhere. And so, that's what this sower does. The goal is maximum harvest.

The sower knows where fruit is most likely to grow up from the seed he sows, but he wants fruit to grow up everywhere, even in the most unlikely places. The goal is fruit. The sower sows to bear fruit and he sows knowing that the seed has the power to bear fruit. The miracle—the power—is not in his sowing, but in the seed he sows.

Now, the human perspective focuses on the wastefulness of the process: Look at all the seed that doesn't bear fruit!

The point of the parable—the point Jesus is making in telling it—reflects a very different perspective: Given all the difficulties and obstacles—all the unfavorable circumstances—how amazing and wonderful that *any* seed bears fruit—and, even more so, that the seed bears so much fruit!

Sowing seeds bears fruit.

But wait a minute—the parables of Jesus are stories about ordinary, everyday stuff that are also, at the same time, about extraordinary, eternal stuff. So let's consider the extraordinary, eternal stuff of this ordinary story.

Who, for instance, is this "sower"? Who is this Who has this amazing fruit-bearing seed—Who is prepared—determined—to spread it everywhere, no matter how unlikely it is to fall on soil that will receive it in a way that will bear fruit?

Well, Jesus, certainly. This is the story of His life and ministry. He has the seed (the good news of the gospel about God's will and plan for our redemption and salvation). And He is determined to share it everywhere. He knows it won't take root everywhere, and He knows why it won't, but He sows the seed everywhere, anyway.

Jesus is the Seed as well, by the way. After all, it is not merely the news about God's love and forgiveness that is imparted to us as knowledge for the mind that bears fruit. This knowledge, when received and believed, transforms us into receptive soil for the Spirit of Jesus Christ to enter into our hearts and germinate a new relationship with God that bears fruit—the fruit of the Spirit.

The Gospel of John says, *"In Him was life, and the life was the light of men."*[207]

That's quite a seed!

John says, *"...to all who received Him...He gave the power to become children of God."*[208]

That's some fruit!

And a part of that fruitfulness is that we, too, become sowers of seed—like Him, scattering the seed of the gospel ourselves across the lives of all kinds of people in all kinds of situations so that the fruit of Christ that has blossomed in us may blossom (through us) in them.

Disciples of Jesus have sown the seed of the gospel in some seemingly hard ground. I discovered last Sunday that gospel seed has been sown in a maximum-security prison down the road a ways. You would think the soil there would be very hard and rocky, with plenty of thorns. But the seed of the gospel has been sown there and it is bearing abundant fruit.

There were seeds sown in Vacation Bible School this week. You can recognize the sowers by the frazzled, exhausted looks on their faces this morning. They sowed seeds everywhere amid the seeming chaos—and the inexperienced observer will wonder how

---

[207] John 1:4, RSV.
[208] John 1:12, RSV.

From Matthew 13

anything could take root in the bedlam of noise and energy that almost a hundred children in these tight spaces created. But this week's sowing will bear remarkable fruit in the days and decades to come.

The sower of gospel seed sows that seed on the golf course and over lunch, at the gym and in the grocery store—not the whole 50-pound bag at one time, of course—but seed sufficient to bear fruit if the soil is receptive.

"But suppose I sow a seed and it falls on deaf ears—hard ground?"

Sow more seed—and sow it in other places. The sower does not test the soil for fruit-bearing potential before he sows.

He just scatters the seed everywhere he can. If he scatters a lot of seed, some of it will bear fruit. And even if it doesn't bear fruit everywhere, it will bear fruit somewhere. And where the seed does bear fruit, the harvest will be tremendous. Sow the seed God has given you. Sow it everywhere you can, and I suspect that God will make sure you never run out of seed to scatter.

And notice how the Sower Jesus sowed the seed. He told stories; He spoke in parables. He said God and His kingdom are like things you see every day and never think about. Jesus said God is like a father who loves and forgives a son (or two) who are disrespectful and selfish and stupid.[209] He said God is like a remarkably compassionate and generous stranger who comes along and puts you back together after the world has beaten you down and left you for dead.[210] The heaven God rules over is like an unexpected treasure, or a jewel so wonderful that you would gladly give up everything else to have it.[211]

Jesus sowed the seed of the gospel—the seed that bears fruit in salvation. He told parables that revealed the sacred in the secular—the divine in the commonplace.

---

[209] Luke 15:11-32.
[210] Luke 10:30-35.
[211] Matthew 13:44-46.

Sowing Seeds—Bearing Fruit

What else are you looking at everyday—that you never think about—but that contains, right there in front of you, some powerful revelation about God and His kingdom? What other parables has God hidden, like treasure in plain sight, to be a seed for growing more spiritual fruit in you?

Jesus spoke in parables to teach us. God has done the same. In fact, you could say that Jesus is God's "parable" about Himself for us. Jesus was a person like you and me—by all outward appearances, a regular human being, fully man. And yet, Paul says in the first chapter of Colossians: in Jesus *"all the fullness of God was pleased to dwell."*[212] Fully man. Fully God.

In Jesus, God says, "You cannot know Me; I am too awesome for you to get your human mind around. But look here at this Man Jesus. That's what I'm like.

"What He says is what I want you to hear about Me. What He does shows you what you need to know about Me. Relating to Him is how you can relate to Me. I have put Myself in Him so that He can be the Seed that, in dying, bears the fruit of your redemption by Me, and your reconciliation with Me."

John writes, *"No one has ever seen God...the only Son, Who is in the bosom of the Father, He has made Him known."*[213]

A sower went out to sow. A simple scene. A familiar figure. A common chore. But is that all?

A Savior went out to sow the Seed of salvation; and even more, an infinite God went out to sow the Seed of a new Creation. Ultimate truth. Breathtaking picture. Song of eternity.

Do you have the ears to hear it?

Do you have the eyes to see it?

Do you have the faith to believe it?

Then sow the seed...and bear the fruit.

---

[212] Colossians 1:19, RSV.
[213] John 1:18, RSV.

Matthew 14:22-33 ESV

²² Immediately [Jesus] made the disciples get into the boat and go on ahead to the other side, while he dismissed the crowds. ²³ And after he had dismissed the crowds, he went up the mountain by himself to pray. When evening came, he was there alone, ²⁴ but by this time the boat, battered by the waves, was far from the land, for the wind was against them. ²⁵ And early in the morning he came walking toward them on the sea. ²⁶ But when the disciples saw him walking on the sea, they were terrified, saying, "It is a ghost!" And they cried out in fear. ²⁷ But immediately Jesus spoke to them and said, "Take heart, it is I; do not be afraid."

²⁸ Peter answered him, "Lord, if it is you, command me to come to you on the water." ²⁹ He said, "Come." So Peter got out of the boat, started walking on the water, and came toward Jesus. ³⁰ But when he noticed the strong wind, he became frightened, and beginning to sink, he cried out, "Lord, save me!" ³¹ Jesus immediately reached out his hand and caught him, saying to him, "You of little faith, why did you doubt?" ³² When they got into the boat, the wind ceased. ³³ And those in the boat worshiped him, saying, "Truly you are the Son of God."

17.

Step Out!

Matthew 14:22-33 ESV

Well! Just when you thought it was safe to go back out on the water…!

It's been less than a month since we saw Jesus calm a storm at sea that all His disciples were sure would sink their little boat—and them. It may have been even less time between that episode and the one you heard about today. Whatever the interval, you just know the disciples have that other incident very much in mind when Jesus walks them to the shoreline and tells them to get back in the boat that brought them there that morning. And in obedience to the One Who calmed the storm and saved their lives, they clamber back over the gunnels of the boat and get themselves organized to row back to wherever they came from.

But when they turn and reach out to help Jesus aboard, they get an unpleasant surprise. He isn't getting in with them. Standing there in the surf, Jesus gives the order to "shove off," and then turns back toward the land—back toward the crowds He must dismiss and the hills behind them that ring the lake.

The disciples are not happy with this unexpected turn of events, but if they say anything to Him, it isn't much. There's no arguing with Jesus. He doesn't take their advice, they've learned. He doesn't take anyone's advice.

The only One Jesus listens to for advice and counsel is His Heavenly Father. And to spend time with His Heavenly Father, in one of those special spiritual prayerful sessions, is what Jesus intends this night. And when His work and the day is done, by whatever light the stars and moon provide, Jesus makes His way up the mountain before Him—up to a private place for prayer.

And while He prays, the disciples put their backs into the business of rowing their boat across the sea. You remember what boats represent for the writers and the readers of the Gospels. The boat is a symbol—a reminder—of the Church. The disciples are in their boat, in obedience to their Master's command.

But it is worth noting that the boat to which Jesus assigns His disciples is no cruise ship—they have not been granted a life of luxury in this boat. Being in the boat calls for hard labor: The winds and waves often work against their reaching the intended destination, even if survival itself is not in question.

And Jesus isn't with them in the boat the way He was when the terrible storm blew up before. They would all feel more comfortable if He were. But even without Jesus in the boat—asleep or awake—the disciples man their stations and carry out their duties. They must, because the sea is so wide and their boat is so small—and far from shore, in the darkness of the night.

※

Their boat is very small when compared to the sea upon which it sails, but it is not so small that there is not a place for you and all the others who have come to call Jesus Lord.

This is the boat of the disciples of Jesus—a symbol for the Church—the vessel into which He has placed all His followers for their safety and for navigating the treacherous waters of life to the destination His Father has prepared.

From Matthew 14

You embark with Jesus on this journey. You join those who, like you, have accepted His invitation to take your place in this vessel, looking for His blessing, and taking up the work that is yours to do.

And sometimes you wonder: "Where is Jesus when the seas are heaving and the winds are howling and the boat is rocking and headway is so very hard to make?"

It's a fair question, and one that was answered for the first disciples in the wee and weariest hours of the morning. After He had spent hours alone in the night, praying, Jesus came to His followers in the boat in a powerful and miraculous way: *"...He came to them, walking on the sea."*

Now, our modern, miracle-proof minds will want to substitute something sweet and inspirational for the Bible's assertion that Jesus has the supernatural ability to overcome the normal laws of nature.

"People don't walk on water. They can't. It isn't possible!"

...which is the point: Jesus is a person, but He is more. Jesus is like every person who ever lived and like *no* person who ever lived. The divine power that Jesus received as a result of His relationship with His Heavenly Father enabled Him to do whatever it took—whatever miracle was necessary—to come to His disciples.

It's a miracle, all right. But like all the miracles of Jesus, it is a miracle with a message: Jesus has the power to overcome any obstacle that would prevent His coming to His disciples.

God has given Jesus the ability to overcome even the roiling, uncontrollable waters of the sea.

The Apostle Paul wrote the Ephesians, *"God placed all things under His feet...."*[214] including, apparently, the waters of the sea. And all this miraculous, nature-overwhelming power is for this simple purpose: so that Jesus can come to you, His disciples. Jesus told

---

[214] Ephesians 1:22, RSV.

Step Out!

His disciples in the Gospel of John, *"I will not leave you as orphans, I will come to you."*[215]

And if something is in the way?

Paul again, to the Romans: *"I am convinced that neither death nor life, neither angels nor demons, neither the present nor the future, nor any powers, neither height nor depth, nor anything else in all creation, will be able to separate us from the love of God that is in Christ Jesus our Lord,"*[216] including, it would seem, the waters that Jesus is able to walk on—waters subject to the authority of the God Who put them in their place at Creation.

Where is Jesus when you need Him?

He is always coming to you. And nothing can stop Him. He is always coming to His disciples in supernatural power.

Of course, it's not always obvious that that's what's happening. Jesus is coming to His disciples in the darkest hour amid a building storm and they don't recognize Him. They fear the worst when they should expect the best.

Ghosts on the water? Phantoms of the deep rising up to haunt them?

No! The Son of God coming near to save them—to save you!

But even when He identifies Himself—even when He makes it clear Who He is and what He's doing, the disciples of Jesus have a hard time replacing their fear with faith.

Of course, we're not just dealing with a "dear, sweet Jesus." This is not just the Jesus Who is kind to little children and gentle with animals.

This is God Incarnate, the One Man in all the world and all of history Who commands the forces of nature that no man can command. Seeing Him stride across the sea in the middle of the night ought to shake you up a little—or a lot. So it takes the disciples a minute to get a grip on themselves as Jesus approaches the boat…

---

[215] John 14:18, KJV.
[216] Romans 8:38-39, RSV.

From Matthew 14

...except that one of them—Peter—has got a grip on something else.

❧

If Jesus has the power to walk on water, Peter thinks, He probably has the power to enable me to walk on water, too. And here's a new wrinkle: Jesus comes to His disciples in the boat—but He is also willing for His disciples to get out of the safety of the boat and come to Him.

"If You are God," shouts Peter above the wind at the Figure in the dark, "tell me (or more accurately) *command* me to come to You."

"*Command* me! Give the order, not just to me to step out of the boat onto the sea, but to the water to hold me up, or to whatever it is that keeps You from sinking when all You've got under You is water."

And Jesus gives the command: "Come!"

And Peter climbs down out of the boat onto—*nothing* that should hold him up. And yet—how firm a foundation![217]

Now, Peter is closer to Jesus than any of the other disciples. Peter has left the security of the boat to go to a whole new place in his relationship with Jesus. One disciple among the 12 recognizes that, for all the blessings of being in the boat, being where Jesus is and doing what Jesus does, regardless of the apparent peril, is infinitely better.

But Peter can't walk on water; and he isn't doing so now. He is walking on whatever power Jesus has put under him to keep him from sinking beneath the waves that, because of Jesus, remain unable to wash over him.

Peter is fully focused on Jesus, and the power to walk on water flows from the-One-Who-can to one who never could have otherwise. And Peter shares a miracle with Jesus—for a moment—

---

[217] George Keith or R. Keen, "How Firm a Foundation," 1787.

Step Out!

for the moment his heart and mind and emotions and faith belong completely to Jesus.

❧

But completely focused faith is so hard to maintain in the face of wind and waves and a world whipping all around you. And so, Peter stopped obeying the command of Jesus. And when he did—when he stopped coming to Jesus in faith—he also stopped receiving the power to walk in that miraculous way—not because Jesus stopped providing it—but because Peter cut the connection through which Jesus was funneling that power to him.

But even that, Jesus could work with, because Peter had stepped out in faith. He had started in faith. In time, Peter would come to the point where he could finish in faith.

But for now, it is enough to know that Jesus came to His disciples, walking on the water—and that one of them, anyway, came to Him the same way—and that all of the disciples came to a deeper understanding of the Person in Whom they had placed their faith, as Peter, and the Jesus Who had just saved him, got in the boat with the rest of them, and they all made their way together to their geographical and spiritual destination.

❧

Jesus has placed you, as His follower, in the Church—a vessel that will see you through a scary world. Sometimes, you are aware of His presence with you. At other times, He seems very far away.

But Jesus is always interceding and advocating for you,[218] coming to you, regardless of the obstacles, inviting you—*commanding* you—to step out of the boat where He put you and, in completely focused faith, come to Him, walking to Him, and *with* Him, in a miraculous way, through the hazards all around you, because He gives you the power to do so.

---

[218] Hebrews 7:24-25; 1 John 2:1.

From Matthew 14

And when you falter—when you see too much of this world and not enough of Him—Jesus reaches out to you and rescues you and returns you to the safety and solace of the fellowship in the boat.

Jesus told Peter, "Come!" And now, when the waves of illness rise up all around you, Jesus comes to you and tells you, "Come!" When you bury a loved one and the waves of grief and loneliness well up within you, Jesus comes to you and bids you, "Come!" When the future terrifies you and your relationships frustrate you, Jesus will come to you and call to you, "Come." And when the work of God's kingdom takes you out of your comfort zone, Jesus comes to you and invites you—*commands* you: "Come."

Step out into the place where you're living your life on the firm foundation Jesus alone provides.

What did He say?

"Be courageous! Don't be afraid! Step out of the boat—and come!"

Walking with Jesus

Matthew 14:22-33 ESV

²² Immediately [Jesus] made the disciples get into the boat and go before him to the other side, while he dismissed the crowds. ²³ And after he had dismissed the crowds, he went up on the mountain by himself to pray. When evening came, he was there alone, ²⁴ but the boat by this time was a long way from the land, beaten by the waves, for the wind was against them. ²⁵ And in the fourth watch of the night he came to them, walking on the sea. ²⁶ But when the disciples saw him walking on the sea, they were terrified, and said, "It is a ghost!" and they cried out in fear. ²⁷ But immediately Jesus spoke to them, saying, "Take heart; it is I. Do not be afraid."

²⁸ And Peter answered him, "Lord, if it is you, command me to come to you on the water." ²⁹ He said, "Come." So Peter got out of the boat and walked on the water and came to Jesus. ³⁰ But when he saw the wind, he was afraid, and beginning to sink he cried out, "Lord, save me." ³¹ Jesus immediately reached out his hand and took hold of him, saying to him, "O you of little faith, why did you doubt?" ³² And when they got into the boat, the wind ceased. ³³ And those in the boat worshiped him, saying, "Truly you are the Son of God."

18.

Walking with Jesus

Matthew 14:22-33 ESV

This is one of those Sundays when I wish you could all speak Greek—or at least read it. I would like to take you back past the English translation of the verses in Matthew 14 that you heard (or have in your Bible), to the original Greek, to the actual, literal words Matthew wrote. Our English versions try to put what was written in a form we can understand. But occasionally, something still gets lost in translation.

As you heard, Jesus has put the disciples in a boat and sent them across the Sea of Galilee where He will meet them later. And, as is often the case, the disciples do not fare well when they are separated from Jesus. Here, they are up to their panic buttons in darkness, difficulty and danger, out in the middle of the stormy sea. (The boat is a symbol for the Church, by the way, and they are safe in the boat where Jesus put them, but they don't seem to realize it.)

They are safe because Jesus is coming to be with them as He promised. It is Jesus Who is coming, and yet they are terrified when they see Him. They are terrified by what they need most—because they do not recognize what they are seeing for What—or Who— It is. There is Jesus in the flesh—the Stiller of storms—the Lord of wind and wave—the Voice of God—the Hand of God—the Son of God—and these 12 men are squealing about phantoms—that's the Greek word Matthew uses. They think He's a ghost.

☙❧

And here's where you really need to know exactly what Matthew wrote. Our English versions say that Jesus tells His disciples, "Take courage! It is I. Don't be afraid." It all sounds very comforting—very reassuring: "It's okay, fellas. It's just Me. Not to worry."

But the Greek doesn't say, "It is I." The Greek words are literally, "εγο ειμι"—"I AM!" It's the same thing God said to Moses when God sent Moses to Egypt. Listen to this part of Exodus, chapter 3:

⁷ Then the LORD *said, "…I will send you…to bring my people, the Israelites, out of Egypt."*

¹³ But Moses said to God, "If I come to the Israelites and say to them, 'The God of your ancestors has sent me to you,' and they ask me, 'What is his name?' what shall I say to them?"

¹⁴ God said to Moses, "I AM WHO I AM." He said further, "Thus you shall say to the Israelites, 'I AM has sent me to you.' ¹⁵ This is my name forever, and this my title for all generations."[219]

Jesus doesn't say, "It is I." Jesus doesn't even say what Moses was to say, "I AM has sent Me to you." Jesus says, "I AM! I am no ghost; I-AM-God!"

And He's walking on water to prove it.

"Take courage!" He says, *"Do not be afraid."* But Jesus is not reassuring the disciples; He's *commanding* them with all the authority of God Himself.

"Take courage?"

---

[219] Exodus 3:7-15, abridged.

From Matthew 14

The Greek word means, "Be bold. Be daring. Trust so completely in Me that your confidence makes you cheerfully take on the greatest challenges." It's a command.

And "Do not fear!"?

That's a command, too. There is always some wind howling around the Christian. The waves are always raging if you're a disciple of Jesus., *"In this world, you will have tribulation...,"*[220] but this is Jesus—this is I AM.

"Do not fear!"

Consider all the things that you do not need to fear because you are under the protection of the One Who spoke the world into existence—Who rules the wind and walks upon the water.

꙰

In our English translations, Peter responds to Jesus, *"If it is You..."*

In the Greek, Peter says to Jesus, *"If You are..."*

"If You are Who You just said You are—if You are God, command me..." "Tell me" isn't strong enough to convey the power of the words Matthew wrote.

Peter does not "offer" to walk to Jesus. He asks Jesus to *make* him walk on the water. If Jesus commands it, it will be so. If it happens, it is only because Jesus, the One Who claims to be I AM, authorizes and empowers it.

And Jesus doesn't suggest or invite or encourage Peter to take a stroll on the sea. He *commands* Him: *"Come!"* "Because I AM, come!"

And Peter does what Jesus commands. Peter obeys because he believes that Jesus is Who Jesus claims to be. And Peter clambers down out of the boat onto the water because he senses something else: What Jesus can do, Jesus can command and empower others to do.

---

[220] John 16:33.

"Come, if you believe that I AM—if you believe that I am God—come and do what I am doing."

Peter was the only one who obeyed the command of Jesus that night—the only one of the disciples to get out of the boat—the only one to know the wonder of walking on the water, even for a moment.

Yes, Peter got distracted by the storm raging around him. But even so, only Peter felt the powerful hand of Jesus lifting him out of the churning water like God the Father would lift Jesus Himself out of death in a borrowed grave.

Peter walked on the water toward Jesus and started to sink, but that wasn't the end of Peter's walking on water. After Jesus took hold of him and lifted him up—saved him—Peter walked back to the boat—safe in the arms of Jesus.

"I AM," said Jesus to a dozen desperate men in a small boat on a large lake.

"If You are…" said one of those men who wanted to experience the power of God.

And when Peter had walked on the water to and with Jesus—and returned with his Lord into a boat that suddenly saw the seas calm and the day breaking sunny and new—they all proclaimed, "You are…! *Truly, You are God's Son!*" Terrified in the night, they are awestruck in the light.

❦

Can you imagine what it was like to do what Peter did? A young lady I know once wrote at a dark and difficult time in her life, "I could never relate to this story before…. I mean: Who walks on water? But now I look back and see the moments when I doubted and sank. Aside from those, I've been walking on water for years."

My people, don't hear this story about Jesus and Peter and try to imagine what it was like. If you're a Christian, you've "been walking on water for years." We've been walking on water as a church, weathering the storms of these past months and stepping

From Matthew 14

out in faith as the great I AM has commanded us. You've been walking on water with every step of faith in obedience to your Lord's commands.

The times when you doubted, you started to sink, just like Peter. But every time you cried out to Jesus, He lifted you up and held you up and walked with you. It only felt like solid ground because He was there, making it so.

"I AM," Jesus says.

There may have been a time when you said to Him, "If You are...." But you've walked with Jesus on too much water, and been rescued from your doubts and fears too many times, and seen Jesus calm too many storms, to do anything now except worship Him and confess, with all His other disciples, that Jesus is Who He says He is: the great I AM—the very Son of God.

And that, praise God, you can do in English—or any other language you chose.

A Question of Identity

Matthew 16:13-20 NRSV

[13] Now when Jesus came into the district of Caesarea Philippi, he asked his disciples, "Who do people say that the Son of Man is?" [14] And they said, "Some say John the Baptist, but others Elijah, and still others Jeremiah or one of the prophets." [15] He said to them, "But who do you say that I am?" [16] Simon Peter answered, "You are the Messiah, the Son of the living God." [17] And Jesus answered him, "Blessed are you, Simon son of Jonah! For flesh and blood has not revealed this to you, but my Father in heaven. [18] And I tell you, you are Peter, and on this rock I will build my church, and the gates of Hades will not prevail against it. [19] I will give you the keys of the kingdom of heaven, and whatever you bind on earth will be bound in heaven, and whatever you loose on earth will be loosed in heaven." [20] Then he sternly ordered the disciples not to tell anyone that he was the Messiah.

19.

A Question of Identity

Matthew 16:13-20 NRSV

Some years ago, someone published a book entitled *Portraits of Jesus*.[221] It is a book of paintings: page after page—one Jesus after another—images through the centuries that really say more about the people who painted them than they do about the One they were trying to portray. Everybody seems to have at least a mental picture of Jesus.

And yet, you could not pick Him out of a line-up. It's not His *face* that sets Jesus apart—that identifies Him. It is His words and His deeds. It is His power and His wisdom, His unity with God and His love for humanity, especially those humans among us the rest of us would reject.

Read the Bible and you will see that people had a lot of opinions about Who Jesus was when He was walking around among them. The same is true today; you can ask anyone. And sometimes, you don't even have to ask. Let someone on an airplane or in a waiting room find out you're a Christian and he'll tell you who he thinks Jesus is—often at great length and with great

---

[221] The book I had in mind when I wrote this sermon may have been *Rembrandt and the Face of Jesus*, Lloyd DeWitt; ed., New Haven, CT: Yale University Press, 2011, though I was given a copy of a similar book many years earlier.

intensity. The picture may be interesting—even imaginative. It will seldom be accurate.

But Jesus Himself raised the question of His identity. Jesus asked His disciples, *"Who do people say that I am?"* Their answers were as I just described: interesting, imaginative—and wrong.

Jesus was the personification of the fears of those who were feeling guilty. Herod killed John the Baptist and figured Jesus was ol' John, come back from the grave.

For others, Jesus was the focus of all their unfulfilled hopes and dreams. He was somebody special (like the Old Testament prophets, especially Elijah and Jeremiah) who were supposed to come along some day with enough God-power to wipe out the bad guys, make everything all right, and take all your problems away.

People were impressed with Jesus, one way or another. Jesus never fails to make an impression. But His goal—His mission—is not to be impressive; it is to impress upon people His true identity.

Unfortunately, people on the "outside" looking in don't see the reality that you can only see in relationship with Jesus. People are always impressed, but to compliment Jesus is not to confess Him.

"What are they saying about Me?" He asked. And the disciples were happy to answer. But Jesus wasn't really interested in the answers to *that* question. "Who do people say that I am?" is really just setting the stage for the truly critical question to come. Knowing what people think about Jesus is useful for understanding our cultural context. It's useful information, but it is not essential in the way the next question will be.

Everything is riding on the next question: the success of the entire Jesus mission—as well as the eternal salvation of Simon and the other disciples. Our salvation today depended on the answer they would give to that question then, just as much as it depends on the answer we give now. If Simon and the others had not given the right answer, we might never have had the chance to answer the question at all.

From Matthew 16

Before they can recount all the possibilities people were suggesting for His identity, Jesus said to His disciples: *"Who do you say I am?"*

And silence reigned. It is one thing to review public opinion; it is quite another to go on record yourself.

"Who do people say that I am?" is conversation, pleasant or otherwise.

"Who do you say I am?" is confrontation—direct and to the point. "Who am I *to you*?" Their tongues were suddenly tied—and yet, this was the most important conversation they would ever have with Jesus.

꙳

Simon could not have answered this question when he started following Jesus. He did not know Who Jesus was then. None of them did.

But in the course of their following Him, they came to realize Jesus was even more—*infinitely* more—than they imagined Him to be when they decided to follow Him in the first place. That's the way it is for all His disciples.

But it's still a tricky question, even for the first disciples. Jesus didn't really fit any of their already established categories. He redefined with His life and ministry all the traditional terms they might have used to identify Him. Jesus was—and remains—more than any term or title we could apply to Him.

But give him credit, Simon decided to take a shot at answering the question. Simon identified Jesus as *"the Christ,"* the long-expected Messiah, the Anointed One sent by God to save the people of God from the power of sin and death, in this life and the next. This, Simon and the others had come to understand, was His function—His purpose.

And, Simon said, Jesus was also *"the Son of the Living God."* The One that God sent was God Himself, divine in the same way that

A Question of Identity

God is divine.[222] This was His essence, which guaranteed that He was a Christ Who had both the authority and the ability to fulfill the mission. Simon said to Jesus, "This is what You have come to do, and this is Who You are."

❦

To identify Jesus as Simon did is to run counter to normal human thinking. While everybody else is working with what they know about Jesus, it turns out that the question of His identity is not ultimately answered by knowing things about Him, but by knowing Him personally. You cannot know His true identity unless you know *Him*.

To know Jesus is to know Who Jesus is. And according to Mathew, to know Who Jesus is is to be blessed. It is to see Jesus and everything else as God wants you to—as God enables you to.

Of course, if you recognize Jesus for Who He is, it will not be through the power of your own perception. *"Flesh and blood"*—human intellect or emotion—will not reveal the true identity of Jesus to you. Only God in heaven will do that. Jesus said to Simon, *"Blessed are you, Simon, son of Jonah, for flesh and blood has not revealed this to you, but my Father who is in heaven."* Without God's divine revelation, these are things you cannot know.[223]

But there's more. When Simon answered the question of Jesus' identity correctly—he settled the question of his own identity as well. The answer you give to the question of His identity answers the question of your identity, too, because we are all, ultimately, who we are in relation to Jesus. We become who we are in relation to Who He is to us.

When Jesus became Christ to Simon, Simon became Peter to—and for—Jesus. Jesus said, "You have told Me that you know Who I am. Now *I* will tell you who *you* are."

---

[222] Colossians 1:19; 2:9.
[223] Deuteronomy 29:29.

From Matthew 16

Is Jesus your Christ? Then you are His "rock," a solid foundation stone in the Church He continues to build, generation after generation. Is He Son of the Living God—God Incarnate—to you? Then you are a "keeper of the keys" to His heavenly kingdom, with the power to open and close the way of salvation to others.

The question of His identity is also the question of your identity. Do you want to know who you are? Decide Who He is to you. You cannot avoid that question forever. Sooner or later, every one of us will answer it, one way or another.[224]

But the question of our identity is not finally for us to decide. Jesus does not say, "Who do you think you are?" The question before us is, "Who do we say Jesus is?" Jesus will define the identity of those who confess Him as Christ. He will reveal to us who and what we are.

But make sure when you answer Him that you answer His question correctly. Jesus is *"the Christ, the Son of the Living God."* Put your will before His and He will merely say, *"I never knew you. Depart from Me...."*[225]

The question of our identity is not really, "Who do we think we are?"—or even "Who do we want to be?"—but "Who does Jesus say we are?"

The question of our identity will be answered for us finally by Jesus, but only after we answer the question of Who He is to us. If we know Him, we will know Who He is. If we know Who He is, we will know who we are. If we know we are His, we will be who He intends for us to be.

---

[224] Philippians 2:9-11.
[225] Matthew 7:23, ESV.

Listen to Jesus

Matthew 17:1-9 ESV

¹ *And after six days Jesus took with him Peter and James, and John his brother, and led them up a high mountain by themselves.* ² *And he was transfigured before them, and his face shone like the sun, and his clothes became white as light.* ³ *And behold, there appeared to them Moses and Elijah, talking with him.* ⁴ *And Peter said to Jesus, "Lord, it is good that we are here. If you wish, I will make three tents here, one for you and one for Moses and one for Elijah."* ⁵ *He was still speaking when, behold, a bright cloud overshadowed them, and a voice from the cloud said, "This is my beloved Son, with whom I am well pleased; listen to him."* ⁶ *When the disciples heard this, they fell on their faces and were terrified.* ⁷ *But Jesus came and touched them, saying, "Rise, and have no fear."* ⁸ *And when they lifted up their eyes, they saw no one but Jesus only.*

⁹ *And as they were coming down the mountain, Jesus commanded them, "Tell no one the vision, until the Son of Man is raised from the dead."*

20.

Listen to Jesus

Matthew 17:1-9 ESV

The Christian life sure has its "ups" and "downs." One minute, you're on the Mount of Transfiguration, dazzled by the divine glory of Jesus. The next, you're hunkered down in remorse as you enter the season of Lent and contemplate the human agony Jesus endured for your sins.

Ash Wednesday is on the schedule for this week, so we'll leave the remorse and agony for a few days. Let's focus on the glory— the picture of a Jesus gathered in a supernatural summit meeting with Moses and Elijah, speaking of things that *"no eye has seen, nor ear heard, nor the heart of man imagined...."*[226]

And then, like a cell phone going off in church, or that patron of the arts who cannot let a softly exquisite passage in a symphony go by without some disruptive gush of emotion, the tranquil and miraculous moment of the Transfiguration is interrupted by that apostolic bull in the spiritual china shop, Simon Peter: "Hey, this is really cool, Lord! How 'bout I go down to Dick's and get some camping gear?"

---

[226] 1 Corinthians 2:9, ESV.

Listen to Jesus

But before Peter can say any more—and you know Peter always has more to say—God Himself speaks the cosmic equivalent of "Hush!"

Peter, James and John—and probably Jesus, Moses and Elijah, too—are surrounded by a cloud that isn't about rain. And a Voice in the cloud, unattached to any body in the cloud, says, "Listen! This Jesus, Who is lit up like the sun, is My Son—My divinely loved and perfectly pleasing Son. Shut up and listen to Him!"

Oh, but how hard that is to do! We want to talk to Jesus. We want to deliver our wish list. We want to "have a little talk with Jesus," as the song goes, so that we can "tell Him all about our troubles."[227]

And that's okay, because the Bible does encourage *"casting all your care upon Him, for He cares for you."*[228] But God also says, "Listen to Jesus."

Here's a question for you to think about: "How often does Jesus get a chance to talk to you?"

Here's another: "How often do you think Jesus has something He wants to tell you?"

Is Jesus waiting for you to pay attention, to listen to Him, or are you waiting for a word from Jesus that never comes? Don't tell me, "I've got prayers that have never been answered?" I'm not asking if you always get what you want—what you ask for. I know the answer to that one.

Do you listen to Jesus? Do you even know what Jesus sounds like? Would you recognize Jesus if He spoke to you?

I've got a Bible at home called a "Red-Letter Edition." It has the words of Jesus printed in bright red. If I want to listen to Jesus, I can read the words in red because they're His words.

But there He is on the Mount of Transfiguration, talking to Moses and Elijah, the ultimate representatives of the Bible's Old Testament Law and Prophets.

---

[227] Cleavant Derricks, "Just a Little Talk with Jesus," c. 1937.
[228] 1 Peter 5:7, NKJV.

Moses said in Deuteronomy, *"God will raise up for you a prophet like me ... you must listen to Him."*[229] You listen to Jesus, not just when you read the words in red, but when you read every word in the Bible. That's why Moses and Elijah were sent to attend to the suddenly spectacular Jesus—and why Moses said, "You must listen to [Jesus]." Jesus has made all the Bible His message.[230]

Is reading the Bible the only way to listen to Jesus? No, but remember, nothing you hear from Jesus in any other way will disagree with what He says in the Bible and what He says by validating the Bible, Old and New, up there on the mountain. If the message doesn't match up, it isn't Jesus you're listening to.[231]

And yet, we listen to a lot of people. We listen to family and friends and neighbors—to elected officials and self-selected celebrities. We listen to anybody who can convince us he or she should be listened to. More and more of these voices try to deny Jesus the right or the undistracted opportunity to speak to you.

But God doesn't tell you to listen to them.

"Listen to My Son," God says. *"Listen to **Him**!"*

What does Jesus have to say?

Oh, He says things like "Get up!" and "Don't be afraid." He said that to His disciples right up there on the mountain.

He said, *"If anyone wishes to come after me, he must deny himself, and take up his cross and follow me,"* just before He took the three disciples up the hill.[232] Jesus has a lot to say, if you will listen. Today, He will say, "This is My Body broken for you" and "this is My Blood shed for you."

Yes, the Christian life sure has its ups and down. But up or down, Jesus has the words of life. And God says, *"Listen to Him."*

---

[229] Deuteronomy 18:15, NIV.
[230] Luke 24:44.
[231] 1 John 4:1, 6.
[232] Matthew 16:24, NASB.

If Your Brother Sins

Matthew 18:15-20 NRSV

[Jesus said:]

[15] "If your brother sins against you, go and tell him his fault, between you and him alone. If he listens to you, you have gained your brother. [16] But if he does not listen, take one or two others along with you, that every charge may be established by the evidence of two or three witnesses. [17] If he refuses to listen to them, tell it to the church. And if he refuses to listen even to the church, let him be to you as a Gentile and a tax collector. [18] Truly, I say to you, whatever you bind on earth shall be bound in heaven, and whatever you loose on earth shall be loosed in heaven. [19] Again I say to you, if two of you agree on earth about anything they ask, it will be done for them by my Father in heaven. [20] For where two or three are gathered in my name, there am I among them."

21.

If Your Brother Sins

Matthew 18:15-20 NRSV

I know you have come today expecting to hear a sermon. Some of you may even be wanting to hear a sermon. You *will* be hearing a sermon. It just won't be the one I thought it was going to be when I provided a title for the bulletin.

I thought the sermon was going to be about the amazing power unleashed when Christians are of one mind before God. I still think that will be a great sermon—and perhaps we'll hear it—someday. But today, the subject of the sermon is sin.

The sin in question is not just any sin, but, according to Jesus, "Christian sin": sin by a Christian against a Christian. Jesus says to His disciples, *"If your brother sins against you, go and tell him his fault, between you and him alone."*

Jesus has been talking about "little ones" and "lost sheep," both images for people who have been brought to salvation and into His Church.

He describes a shepherd who goes after a sheep that strays and rejoices when he finds it. "God," He says, "does not want even one person brought into the Church to be lost."[233] And then He

---

[233] Luke 15:4-7.

says, *"If your brother sins against you...."* Jesus is talking about our spiritual brother—or sister—a Christian who is now family, a fellow member of the Church Jesus established to continue His work and be His Body on earth.

Unfortunately, Christians do sin, even after accepting the saving, transforming grace of God. Little ones get lost and sheep go astray, even in the Church. Christians even sin against other Christians.

So Jesus tells His disciples, *"If your brother sins against you, go and tell him his fault,"* and then Jesus lays out a whole sequence of actions. It sounds like great advice—a superb system for conflict resolution.

⁂

But that's not the point.

The emphasis for Jesus is not, *"If your brother sins against you...."* His concern is *"If your brother sins...."*

It's not about resolving conflicts between Christians, it's about restoring a Christian brother or sister whose behavior has damaged his or her relationship with Christ and the fabric of the Christian fellowship.

Jesus is not instructing you about how to get an apology or compensation—deserved or otherwise. It's not really about *you* at all. As far as your side of things is concerned, if you are sinned against, Jesus is very clear: forgive the sin and move on.

If we had read a few more verses this morning, you would have heard Jesus tell Peter to forgive 77 times (or 70 times 7 times, depending on your translation).[234] You would lose count long before you got there—and lose interest, too, probably—which is what Jesus had in mind.

Deal with your hurt or angry feelings in the light of God's grace to you. You have been forgiven much. Do the same.[235] How *you*

---

[234] Matthew 18:21-22.
[235] Luke 7:47.

From Matthew 18

feel—the emotional and psychological impact of this sin on *you*—is not the issue. Restoration of a lost sheep to the fold is.

As for the physical or financial damage done to you by another Christian's sin against you: Take it up with God. God will take care of you. He can and will comfort you and redeem the damage done to you.[236]

❧❧

"If your brother sins against you...." The point here is not that you are the victim of the sin, but that you are the witness to the sin.

The focus is on the fact that you are aware that a Christian brother or sister has sinned. Because the sin was committed against you, you are the one who knows the moral and spiritual risk this disciple of Christ has incurred. You are the one who sees that the person is out of the will of God.

Your knowledge of that fact makes you responsible—not to get personal satisfaction for the wrong done to you—but to do all in your power to bring this Christian back from rebellion against God, and to restore him or her to obedience before God and harmony with the fellowship of believers. That's why you are the one to go—because you know.

Jesus does not say, "Go to your brother and 'tell him off,'" but *"go to him and tell him his sin."* Go and tell him as one who has also sinned—and may sin again. Go in humility and in love.

❧❧

When His enemies crucified Him, Jesus prayed, *"Forgive them, Father, for they know not what they do."*[237] But, of course, the Christian does know. The Christian has heard and believed the gospel. The Christian has claimed the grace of God in Christ Jesus that saves from sin and ensures eternal life.[238]

---

[236] Genesis 50:15-21.
[237] Luke 23:34, RSV.
[238] Ephesians 2:8-9.

If Your Brother Sins

Christians are those who, in the words of the Book of Hebrews, *"have once been enlightened, who have tasted the heavenly gift, and have become partakers of the Holy Spirit, and have tasted the goodness of the word of God and the powers of the age to come...."*[239]

If a Christian has sinned and has not acknowledged it—confessed it—repented of it—and sought to make amends for it—the sin will do harm to the sinning brother and to the Church.

It will weaken his relationship with God, his effectiveness as a Christian, the health and effectiveness of the Church as the Body of Christ, and his witness for Christ in the world. Sin left unrepented will extend the trajectory of a Christian's rebellion to other and greater sins.

We as Christians are to care so much about the spiritual condition of our brother or sister that we will take on the awkwardness, the embarrassment, the inconvenience, the potential hostility and misunderstanding that comes with going to that person and laying out the case as we see it.

"If he listens to you..."—takes you seriously—takes whatever action is appropriate—*"you have gained your brother...."*

But not for yourself.

You have gained him for Christ and for His Church. You have restored this person to the relationships that were damaged by his sin.

If he does not listen, his problem is not with you, but with Christ. If you have gone representing Christ rather than yourself, his response to you is not "personal," however he may intend it—or you may experience it. If he tells you to "pack sand" (as we say in the military), *"the peace of God which passes all understanding will keep your heart and mind in Christ Jesus."*[240] You'll be okay.

---

[239] Hebrews 6:4-5, RSV.
[240] Philippians 4:7, RSV.

From Matthew 18

If your brother sins against you, go and tell him his fault, as a service to Christ and His Church—as an act of love toward a brother who has sinned—to restore him to Christ and the Church.

To do otherwise is to disobey the command of Christ in Scripture, to allow a Christian brother or sister to drift further away from our Savior and Lord, to weaken the work and witness of the Church, and—in the final analysis—to sin yourself—against Christ and against His Church, and against the one who sinned against you.

Romans 14:3-11 ESV

³ Let not the one who eats despise the one who abstains, and let not the one who abstains pass judgment on the one who eats, for God has welcomed him. ⁴ Who are you to pass judgment on the servant of another? It is before his own master that he stands or falls. And he will be upheld, for the Lord is able to make him stand.

⁵ One person esteems one day as better than another, while another esteems all days alike. Each one should be fully convinced in his own mind. ⁶ The one who observes the day, observes it in honor of the Lord. The one who eats, eats in honor of the Lord, since he gives thanks to God, while the one who abstains, abstains in honor of the Lord and gives thanks to God. ⁷ For none of us lives to himself, and none of us dies to himself. ⁸ For if we live, we live to the Lord, and if we die, we die to the Lord. So then, whether we live or whether we die, we are the Lord's. ⁹ For to this end Christ died and lived again, that he might be Lord both of the dead and of the living.

¹⁰ Why do you pass judgment on your brother? Or you, why do you despise your brother? For we will all stand before the judgment seat of God; ¹¹ for it is written,

"As I live, says the Lord, every knee shall bow to me, and every tongue shall confess to God."

Unity, Liberty, Charity

Matthew 18:21-35 ESV

²¹ Then Peter came up and said to [Jesus], "Lord, how often will my brother sin against me, and I forgive him? As many as seven times?" ²² Jesus said to him, 'I do not say to you seven times, but seventy-seven times.

²³ "Therefore the kingdom of heaven may be compared to a king who wished to settle accounts with his servants. ²⁴ When he began to settle, one was brought to him who owed him ten thousand talents ²⁵ And since he could not pay, his master ordered him to be sold, with his wife and children and all that he had, and payment to be made. ²⁶ So the servant fell on his knees, imploring him, 'Have patience with me, and I will pay you everything.' ²⁷ And out of pity for him, the master of that servant released him and forgave him the debt. ²⁸ But when that same servant went out, he found one of his fellow servants who owed him a hundred denarii, and seizing him, he began to choke him, saying, 'Pay what you owe.' ²⁹ So his fellow servant fell down and pleaded with him, 'Have patience with me, and I will pay you.' ³⁰ He refused and went and put him in prison until he should pay the debt. ³¹ When his fellow servants saw what had taken place, they were greatly distressed, and they went and reported to their master all that had taken place. ³² Then his master summoned him and said to him, 'You wicked servant! I forgave you all that debt because you pleaded with me. ³³ And should not you have had mercy on your fellow servant, as I had mercy on you?' ³⁴ And in anger his master delivered him to the jailers, until he should pay all his debt. ³⁵ So also my heavenly Father will do to every one of you, if you do not forgive your brother from your heart."

22.

Unity, Liberty, Charity

Romans 14:3-11; Matthew 18:21-35 ESV

We are an interdenominational church. It says so, right on our logo—right under our name. It's in small letters—you'll probably need a magnifying glass to see it on the back of your bulletin—but it's there: "Trinity Christian Fellowship—An Interdenominational Church."

And we put that "identifier" there right at the very beginning—right from the start.

Right from the start, we decided to be different—we decided to be a fellowship of Christians who agree to disagree.

And we do disagree—about a lot of things. You have to, if some are going to be Baptists, and some Catholics, and others Methodists and Lutherans and Presbyterians and Episcopalians and whatever else, and some nothing at all because they—*you*—have never had a label or you've tried most all of them at one time or another, and didn't like how they fit.

People who don't know us have asked me, "What's Trinity's position on this issue?" or "What does your church believe about 'that'?"

Well, first of all, it's not *my* church. But more importantly, I have to tell them, "We've probably got a lot of positions on that issue," and "I'd have to ask around to see what all we believe about that particular doctrine or interpretation."

Each denomination has nailed down its unique beliefs for its adherents—in many cases, a long time ago. But we're a little bit of all of them—we have some of all of these denominations represented in our fellowship—so we're something of a patchwork quilt theologically.

"But how can you do that? How could that possibly work?"

The only way it can work is the way Paul told the Christians in the church in Rome to make it work. He said, "Do everything to be unified and nothing to be uniform."

When you join a church—or start one—the natural tendency is to expect that you will agree with the rest of the people—and they, with you. And when you discover you don't agree with somebody about something—and sooner or later you will discover that—it can really bother you. The natural tendency is to try to get everybody to agree—which usually means trying to get "them" to agree with "us"—since, after all, "we" are obviously right.

Now, we do agree about a lot of things. I think we agree about the important things; we are unified by our shared commitment to the essence of Christianity, otherwise, we could not cope with not agreeing about so many other things. But disagreeing is still uncomfortable—and has its risks.

The church in Rome had disagreements. And their disagreements were causing factions—threatening their spiritual unity. And even though it wasn't Paul's church—he had not founded it or even visited it—he was willing to talk to them about how to deal with their differences. And he did so in an interesting way.

Paul labeled the factions. But he did not call them "right" or "wrong." He called them the "weak" and the "strong." And here's where it gets interesting: contrary to what you might expect, he called the more devout ones—the ones who sacrificed more and worked harder to practice their faith—the "weak" ones. Those who didn't do a lot to distinguish themselves from the rest of the world, Paul labeled the "strong"—and appears to have placed himself squarely in their camp.

"But that can't be right! Surely, the people who put more effort into being Christians are better Christians. Surely, they're the 'strong' Christians."

Not according to Paul. The way Paul sees it, being a Christian is not, first of all, about what you do, but about how "strongly" you believe that Jesus Christ has done all that needs to be done for you to make you right with God and free from the condemnation of sin. The "strong" are those who are able to believe that Jesus made everything okay. The "weak" are those who "believe," but feel the need to hedge their bets just a bit by submitting themselves to special diets and paying special attention to special days on the calendar, just in case God cares about those things.

༄༅

Now, Paul may also have called the "strong" the "strong" because there were more of them in the church than the others. It appears that they were in the majority, because most of what Paul says about preserving the unity of the church, he says to them.

Paul says, "Accept the weaker folks into the church—welcome them—and not just so that you can harass them for being different from you. Respect them—and the things that make them different from you."

But preserving the unity of the church is not just the responsibility of some of the members. It's everybody's job—however you go about "doing" your Christianity.

To the more devout and self-sacrificing believers, Paul says, "No judging the easy-going guys as deficient in faith or spiritual maturity. They belong to God and God will judge them—just as you belong to God and God will judge you."

And here's some good news for "strong" and "weak" alike, if you're willing to hear it: God accepts you both. God accepts you both, not because you're right in how you've decided to practice your faith, but because, however you're practicing it, you're doing what you believe will please God—you want to please God. And when you share that desire—that commitment—you are unified in Christ—the "strong" with the "weak"—whatever your differences.

❧

"But do you know how aggravating it is to show up for a pot luck supper at church and see these guys turn their noses up at our food because it's not good enough—not pure enough—for them?"

"And every time we turn around, we're looked down on because we shouldn't be out having some good clean fun on some day they decided was holy?"

"Yeah? Well, we're trying to live dedicated Christian lives in this moral cesspool of a city—to be good witnesses for the gospel—and people in our own church act like we are lunatics and live like the ways of the world around us are really just fine."

And Paul says, "Yes! You're different. Now, get along! Both sides are saved. Both sides are acceptable to God. Both of you are doing what you're doing as your best effort to honor God. Respect and accept each other as the servants of God you all are—for the unity of the Body that is more important to God than what any of you is doing."

"But how?"

❧

Maybe what Jesus told Peter applies here: Practice repeated forgiveness. Every time you're exasperated, give your aggravation to God and your forgiveness and forbearance to your Christian brother or sister. Ask yourself, "What is God doing in these folks whose behavior bothers me so much?" And then ask yourself,

"What is God doing in me as I deal with these folks whose behavior bothers me so much?"

In Rome, they were getting worked up over things like whether meat should be on the Christian menu and when and how to hold a religious holiday. For Christians today, we can divide up sides over equaling pressing matters like what to wear to church and what kind of music to sing when we get here and where should we put the words for you to sing (or not sing) by. Churches break up over what version of the Bible to read and what color the carpets should be. Sooner or later, we're actually going to get to decide where to build our church and how to pay for it.

Whatever side you chose on any of these or other issues, you will have a reason that is compelling for you. The same will be true for those who disagree with you. And none of that releases you, or any of us, from our obligation to God to preserve the unity of our fellowship.

Fortunately, whether we are right or wrong—weak or strong—because we are committed to the unity of the Body—we are all growing deeper in faith and closer to Christ. Though there are differences in the way we practice our faith, we allow room for each other to grow and encourage one another in the un-uniform process, so that we all move forward—often out of step—but always advancing together to the glorious goal God has set for us all in Christ Jesus.

That's why we use the maxim of the Protestant Reformation leader Philip Melanchthon to describe how we "do church":

>"In Essentials: Unity;
>
>In Non-essentials: Liberty;
>
>In All Things: Charity"

Unity—liberty—charity—Trinity. There is something to be said for an interdenominational church—if it's a fellowship where the "weak" and the "strong" will live lovingly with one another, despite their inevitable differences.

Vineyard Work and Vineyard Wages

Matthew 20:1-16 ESV

[Jesus said:]

¹ "For the kingdom of heaven is like a master of a house who went out early in the morning to hire laborers for his vineyard. ² After agreeing with the laborers for a denarius a day, he sent them into his vineyard. ³ And going out about the third hour he saw others standing idle in the marketplace, ⁴ and to them he said, 'You go into the vineyard too, and whatever is right I will give you.' ⁵ So they went. Going out again about the sixth hour and the ninth hour, he did the same. ⁶ And about the eleventh hour he went out and found others standing. And he said to them, 'Why do you stand here idle all day?' ⁷ They said to him, 'Because no one has hired us.' He said to them, 'You go into the vineyard too.' ⁸ And when evening came, the owner of the vineyard said to his foreman, 'Call the laborers and pay them their wages, beginning with the last, up to the first.' ⁹ And when those hired about the eleventh hour came, each of them received a denarius. ¹⁰ Now when those hired first came, they thought they would receive more, but each of them also received a denarius. ¹¹ And on receiving it they grumbled at the master of the house, ¹² saying, 'These last worked only one hour, and you have made them equal to us who have borne the burden of the day and the scorching heat.' ¹³ But he replied to one of them, 'Friend, I am doing you no wrong. Did you not agree with me for a denarius? ¹⁴ Take what belongs to you and go. I choose to give to this last worker as I give to you. ¹⁵ Am I not allowed to do what I choose with what belongs to me? Or do you begrudge my generosity?' ¹⁶ So the last will be first, and the first last."

23.

Vineyard Work and Vineyard Wages

Matthew 20:1-16 ESV

Tomorrow is Labor Day. And today, Jesus tells a Labor Day story, a story in which work and wages are handled very differently than you would expect in our world of organized labor and contract wages. But then, His story is not about this world; it's about a reality He calls "the kingdom of heaven."

Jesus says, *"The kingdom of heaven is like a landowner who went out early in the morning to hire men to work in his vineyard."*

Notice that Jesus does not say this kingdom *"will* be like...." The kingdom of heaven is not something that will come into existence someday. It exists now. But like the holiday in a long weekend, the kingdom of heaven is easily overlooked as we focus on the things of this material world. Still, the kingdom of heaven is here today, just the same.

Jesus knows that all of us will have to deal with the kingdom of heaven, sooner or later. All of us, sooner or later, will submit to its authority and be subject to the kingdom's way. And Jesus paints us a picture of this kingdom and its King—and shows us that things are different in this kingdom because this is a different kind of King. And here's a hint: Don't be surprised when the landowner in the story turns out to be God and the vineyard, God's kingdom.

Vineyard Work and Vineyard Wages

The first part of the story has to do with work—work in the vineyard. The one who planted, nurtured, and owns the vineyard has decided to recruit workers to help him with the work. *He* takes the initiative. No one comes into his vineyard unless he has sought him out and sent him. And no one is sent into the vineyard just to enjoy it. Everyone in the vineyard is expected—is *sent*—to do "vineyard work."

The vineyard work is so important to the landowner that he goes out early in the morning to find workers to send into his vineyard. It is his first priority.

It is so important that he agrees to the terms demanded by this first group of men hired to work throughout the day. These laborers do not agree to *his* terms; *he* agrees to *theirs*: for a full day's work, they demand a full day's wages—no more, no less.

But we'll talk about vineyard wages later.

❧

Vineyard work is not just the landowner's top priority; it is his ongoing concern. Throughout the day, he returns repeatedly to the place where potential workers are to be found and sends all who will go, into the vineyard. Perhaps they cannot accomplish as much as those who have been in the field longer. He does not investigate their ability to do the work well. He simply says to all, *"...go and work in my vineyard."*

Even when it's so late in the day that it shouldn't be worth the effort to send anybody else into the vineyard, the landowner seems almost obsessed with getting every worker in there he can: *"You, also, go and work in my vineyard,"* he says to the eleventh-hour workers. It appears that, as long as day lasts, there is work—vital work—to be done in this particular vineyard. *Everyone* is called to vineyard work.

"So what is 'vineyard work'?"

It is *kingdom* work.

"All right then, what is 'kingdom' work?"

From Matthew 20

It is the purpose for the kingdom. It is what the kingdom exists to produce. A vineyard exists to produce a harvest. A kingdom that is like a vineyard exists to produce of harvest of its own, though its fruit is necessarily different. The harvest of the kingdom of heaven is citizens of the kingdom—faithful, obedient citizens, loyal and joyful subjects of their King. Harvesting these citizens for this kingdom is the first priority of its King. It is the work to which He recruits all who will accept His call.

So where is this heavenly vineyard? Where do you go when you accept His commission to 'go and work in His vineyard'?

You go wherever He sends you, of course, but mostly you go wherever you've *been* going, except now you discover that you aren't just going to your work, or your club, your school, or your chores. Your job is to work in His vineyard. What you do and where you go each day is where the vineyard is—because that's where the harvest is.

Just doing your job? Just working your daily "to do" list? God says, *"Go and work in My vineyard.* Go wherever you go every day, and while you're there, work in My vineyard."

Wherever you are, whatever you're doing, you're not just there to do what you do there; you're there to do vineyard work—kingdom-of-heaven work—if you're willing.

"But I'm not a very good harvester."

That's okay, the landowner doesn't seem too concerned about the credentials or expertise of the workers.

"But I've never done any vineyard work where I go every day."

Then it's time to get started. The landowner sends some of the workers into the vineyard long after when they should have gotten started. Wherever you are in your life today, whatever you're doing with the time you've got left on this earth, God is calling you to go wherever it is you go and work in the vineyard—to turn your effort and your attention to kingdom business.

Vineyard Work and Vineyard Wages

Of course, Labor Day is not just about work; it's also about wages. And the story Jesus tells about the vineyard moves from vineyard work to vineyard wages as well. Jesus says that, at the end of the day, the landowner "settles up" with the workers. But if his commitment to the harvest seemed obsessive, his compensation for those who labor in the vineyard will seem absurd.

No one is cheated by the landowner, but the wage is unexpectedly generous for some. Everybody gets what he needs, regardless of his hours in the vineyard.

The problem comes when the workers start comparing compensation. Those with "longevity" or "seniority" in the vineyard work are upset to see others get as much as they do.

But the landowner has done them no harm—except to undermine their ability to look down on others and enjoy a sense of superiority. But before you criticize what he gives anybody, remember this: the first bunch made a different bargain with the landowner than did those who came into the vineyard later in the day.

Some workers came to the vineyard early and worked throughout the long, hot day. But these men also happened to have set the terms by which they would work for the landowner—and he agreed to their terms. Those who worked with an expectation of a wage received the wage agreed upon—and were then unhappy because the landowner kept his end of the bargain. They drove a hard bargain and got everything they demanded—and were much the worse for it. They chose to do *vineyard* work for *worldly* wages.

❧

But there was a different approach. The other workers were called to vineyard work on the basis of a simple promise. They were invited to work in the vineyard *in faith*, trusting that the owner would take care of them properly. They worked. And the landowner kept his promise. And they discovered that his idea of "right" went far beyond theirs—and they were much the better for

From Matthew 20

it. They were not *paid*; they were *blessed*, far beyond any reasonable expectation. They received what you might call "vineyard wages."

The first group, who chose to do vineyard work for worldly wages, saw the incredible result of the other approach and felt they have suffered at the hand of the owner: "Others are getting more than they deserve; so should we!" In other words: "I deserve more than I deserve!"

But they got what they *bargained* for—because they chose to bargain. In fact, the only one who actually "suffered" as a result of this amazing demonstration of generosity was the owner himself. He paid a full day's wage to many who didn't—couldn't—give him a full day's work in return. But that's just his way of doing business—vineyard business—kingdom business.

❦

So what are we to make of this "Labor Day story" Jesus tells?

There is a work and a wage unlike anything we know on earth. We are called to see in everything we do the possibility—the opportunity—to engage in kingdom work, bringing in the harvest that is more important to God than anything. Vineyard work—kingdom work—is a work people are called to; no one goes to the vineyard unbidden. It is a work God continues to call us to, no matter how late in the day (or in our own lives) we hear the call—or how long we delay before we respond to it. This work is so important to God that it does not matter if we aren't particularly good at it, as long as we are willing to go and do it.

But by our willingness to go and work *in faith*, on the basis of the King's promise alone, our work becomes not just our side of a negotiated contract, it is transformed into a commitment we share with the One Who calls us to the work.

We become more than servants, more than employees, more than part of a labor force fulfilling contract obligations. We become the beloved children of the vineyard Owner. We become the heirs of the kingdom—with all the assets of the kingdom at our disposal. In the kingdom of heaven, the servants are citizens, and the citizens are adopted sons and daughters of the King. This King does not parcel out payments in this kingdom; He pours out blessings upon all who will do the kingdom's work in faith.

That is the true vineyard wage. It is the only kingdom wage. Those who reject it in favor of worldly wages reject their proper place in God's kingdom. They, sadly, relate to God by contract and get what (and *only* what) they bargain for.

In the kingdom of heaven, every day is Labor Day and every day, the King is recruiting workers for the kingdom. He calls you to kingdom work and offers you kingdom wages.

The King is calling.

What will you do?

24.

It's Not Fair!

Matthew 20:1-16 ESV (p. 166)

It's not fair; it's just not fair!" The crowd gathers and, in their shared surprise and disappointment, the complaint gathers steam: "It's just not fair, I tell you!"

They all did what they were expected to do—what they had agreed to do. But at the end of the day, when the final reckoning was announced, the result certainly wasn't what they had expected. The numbers weren't right. They felt cheated. They saw others getting what they had been promised—what the others surely didn't deserve—and the people in the crowd got angry. "This outcome is not fair!"

I am referring, of course, to the story Jesus tells about a landowner who hires a bunch of day laborers to work in his vineyard.

☙❧

We just want what's fair. What's wrong with that? What's wrong with "fair"?

Let's start with what's right with it. It would seem logical that for decent, honest, law-abiding people, fair is better than unfair. It would seem that justice is preferable to injustice. Due process of

It's Not Fair!

law is surely an improvement over corruption, manipulation and all manner of insult and injury. The idea of what's fair—the idea that everybody deserves a fair deal—is certainly a step up from savagery and the unprincipled exercise of power for personal gain. An eye for an eye, and a tooth for a tooth? Now, that's fair. And it was a good idea when the common practice was a life (or two or ten or ever how many you could take) for anything you didn't much like.

❧

But the concept of "fair" is a problem because it is a subjective thing. Our individual ideas about what is fair are based on our own individual value systems. Your idea of what's fair and mine may differ widely, even if we are both deeply committed to being fair. And there seem to be different levels or degrees of fairness. We talk about something being "fair enough," or something else being "more than fair." It doesn't really help us to say, "Fair's fair," if we can't agree in the pinch about just what "fair" is. "Fair" isn't a particularly useful marker if it's always moving around to satisfy the whims of those who are using it.

And we do use it. We use the idea of fairness to hold onto what we've got when there's a risk of losing it. We emphasize fairness to get *something* when we risk getting nothing. "Fair" is the flag we raise to get more, when we risk getting less. "Fair" is about minimizing our risk in a world we cannot totally control.

You see, in addition to being subjective, our ideas about fairness are also rooted in self-centeredness. "Fair" is about our desire to protect our own interest—to get our share—and to get *all* of our share. We tend to want to get the maximum of fairness for ourselves and our side, while carefully measuring out the barest minimum of fairness to anybody and everybody else. The all-day workers got what they were told they would get, which you would think was fair. But they were angry—they felt themselves unfairly

From Matthew 20

treated—when they discovered other people had received just as much for less work. To them, the landowner wasn't fair.

❧

But this raises another problem with the idea of fairness. Jesus is telling a parable here. He's explaining what the kingdom of heaven is like. So the landowner clearly represents God, which is a reasonable analogy, since *"the earth is the Lord's and the fullness thereof."*[241] But please notice that Jesus is telling us that God is not "fair," not by our standards.

Oh, God is good to us. But He's just as good to everybody else. He causes the rain to fall on the just and the unjust alike.[242]

But the unjust don't deserve it. He gives the same reward—the same blessing—to the all-day workers as He does to the last-minute workers. And we don't like it, not one bit. It's like going to a party and seeing other women wearing your dress and knowing they got theirs at a discount store. God is not "fair."

❧

And that's true. What God is, is merciful. And He is merciful to all. God has raised grace to a more important place than justice in His dealings with us, and He wants us to do the same thing in our dealings with others. God is remarkably generous. How amazing that we are so ready to "recount the votes" to see if God's generosity is fair. If we are determined to demand fairness out of life, we're going to live in conflict with a generous God Who is less committed to fairness (as we subjectively define it) than we are.

Is God's generosity fair? Of course it's not fair! It's generosity, for Christ's sake. Generosity isn't supposed to be fair; it's better than fair. Fair is better than unfair, if—*if*—there is no mercy, no grace, no generosity involved. But God gives infinitely more than

---

[241] Psalm 24:1, KJV.
[242] Matthew 5:45.

a fair wage. There are no wages with God; there are only gifts, wonderful gifts of grace.

So Jesus puts our interest in "fairness" and our interest in generosity in unavoidable conflict so that we cannot live comfortably with our own ideas about the one (fairness) that make the other (generosity) functionally impossible. He wants us to develop what one of my friends calls "an attitude of gratitude."

Stop worrying about the pecking order and the payoff for the kingdom of God. Reorient your perspective. If your idea of a thing is different from God's idea of a thing, that's probably a good indication that you might ought to reconsider your idea of the thing.

Do we *deserve* God's blessings more than other people?

How can you "deserve" a blessing? On the other hand, how can you despise a blessing just because it wasn't sufficiently better than someone else's blessing? God causes the rain to fall on the just and the unjust alike. "But the unjust don't deserve it!" And neither do the just who, as it turns out, are also unjust. They just won't admit it, or don't realize it.

༺༻

In a Special Olympic program, all the contestants were lined up, ready to start the race. When the gun went off, one of the runners lost her balance and fell down within a few feet of the starting line. And then an unusual thing happened. All the other runners stopped and waited for her to get up and catch up. When she was back with the pack, they all finished the race together. It wasn't fair, by our standards, but it was generous. And as far as they were concerned, everybody won.

But these were all handicapped children, you say. Well, we're all God's children, as I recall. And who is to say whether their mental and physical handicaps are worse than our moral and spiritual ones?

From Matthew 20

Last week, I said that God wasn't worried about the money; it was the principle of the thing. Here, at the end of the day, for these who have worked the hardest and the longest—for these who await their reward—who have watched an amazing and unexpected exhibition of unmerited generosity, it is about the money.

But Jesus is trying to draw our attention back to the principle of the thing. Will the laborers allow the landowner to change their minds about the fairness of what he has done? Will we allow God to convert our view about generosity so that it conforms to His view? God wants people to help Him in the harvest; God wants us to share His values and His goals. God wants us to forego the safety and comfort of fairness for the glory of generosity.

If "fair" is the best you can do, then, yes, be fair. But is that really what you want? Is it what God wants? God can do so much better than "fair," and, Jesus says, so can you. Accept God's generosity to you. Accept that God will be generous to all. Imitate His generosity in all you do.

Make fairness your creed and you'll often be frustrated. Make generosity your goal and you'll never be thwarted. God has chosen grace over law, mercy over justice, generosity over fairness.

What will you choose?

Rendering

Matthew 22:15-22 NRSV

¹⁵ Then the Pharisees went and plotted to entrap him in what he said.

¹⁶ So they sent their disciples to him, along with the Herodians, saying,

"Teacher, we know that you are sincere, and teach the way of God in accordance with truth, and show deference to no one; for you do not regard people with partiality. ¹⁷ Tell us, then, what you think. Is it lawful to pay taxes to the emperor, or not?" ¹⁸ But Jesus, aware of their malice, said, "Why are you putting me to the test, you hypocrites? ¹⁹ Show me the coin used for the tax." And they brought him a denarius. ²⁰ Then he said to them, "Whose head is this, and whose title?" ²¹ They answered, "The emperor's." Then he said to them, "Give therefore to the emperor the things that are the emperor's, and to God the things that are God's."

²² When they heard this, they were amazed; and they left him and went away.

25.

Rendering

Matthew 22:15-22 NRSV

The question was about taxes. But the issue wasn't. The issue was the will of God.

They asked Jesus, "Is it 'lawful' (meaning: 'permitted by God's Law in the Bible') to pay taxes to a government we despise—a government that does not share our faith or respect our spiritual values?"

They, of course, have no respect for the independence, integrity and spiritual insight they acknowledge Jesus has. Perhaps they should have asked, "Is it okay with God for us to call You 'Teacher' when we have no intention of learning anything from You—when we plan to use whatever You say as a weapon against You?"

But the Bible says what the Bible says, and we ought not go changing it, no matter how much better we think we could make it—or how much more convenient it would be for us if we did.

So the question is, "Jesus, what do you think? Is it lawful to pay taxes to Caesar?"[243]

---

[243] The word in the original Greek text is "Καίσαρος"—Kaisaros—Caesar.

Rendering

It's a devilish question. If He says "Yes," it looks like a compromise of spiritual commitment that will destroy His credibility with the crowds. If He says "No," it sounds like rebellion and will cost Him His freedom and perhaps His life. Either way, His enemies will be happy. "Go ahead, Jesus: 'yes' or 'no'?"

They set the trap and offer the bait. Jesus acknowledges the trap and takes the bait, springing the trap—and leaving His enemies wondering how *they* got caught in the seemingly perfect snare they had set for Him.

It turns out that Jesus really is a Teacher, in addition to everything else. And He will use even a deceitful question from malicious enemies to teach an important lesson about God and God's will for us.

❦

The lesson is about "rendering."

"Render" is the traditional translation of the word Jesus used to answer their question about paying taxes. It's a better translation than "give," because rendering is more than giving.

Giving is voluntary. It's a free choice. It may even be an act of grace. Rendering, on the other hand, is fulfilling an obligation or surrendering what is due to one who has authority or power over you.

Jesus says, *"Render to Caesar the things that are Caesar's..."*[244] "If you owe the taxes, pay the taxes."

But Jesus really isn't interested in what you render to the government, except to say that there are limits to what is due any power (governmental or otherwise) in this world. There are limits to your rendering to Caesar, because there is a rendering that God requires. It is *this* rendering to God that really concerns Jesus because what you render to God is what really matters.

---

[244] Matthew 22:21, ESV.

From Matthew 22

Jesus says, "Show Me the money you use to pay this tax. Bring Me one of the government's coins and let Me look at it." And somebody hustles off to find one since Jesus, apparently, doesn't have one of His own. When they return with the coin, they hand it over to Him. Jesus looks at the coin and then asks: "Whose image is this?" "Whose likeness is stamped on this coin?"

༄༅

The Greek word for "likeness" is "εἰκὼν" or "icon." It's the same word Paul will use in Romans when he says that God conforms believers to the *image* of His Son.[245] And when he says in Colossians that this Son is the *image* of the invisible God,[246] the word Paul uses is "icon." Christ is the very *image* of God, and we, by the grace of God, bear the *image* of Christ on us.[247] That's what God had in mind at the culmination of Creation when He said, *"Let us make man in our **image**, after our likeness..."*[248]

And whose image is on the coin?

Just some guy in Rome who is running the Roman Empire for a while.

"And whose inscription is written on the coin?" Jesus says, turning it over in His hand.

You know what's inscribed on our coins: "In God We Trust." On the coin they gave Jesus was written the identity of the Roman ruler. His title was "Caesar." His name was "Tiberius." He claimed on the coin to be the son of a god, and to be the religious leader of all the world. He was a powerful man—at the time. But he was not as powerful as he claimed to be on the coin. He's long dead now and all but forgotten. When he inscribed his title on his coins, his intended message was clear: "Wherever this coin goes, I rule!"

---

[245] Romans 8:29.
[246] Colossians 1:15.
[247] 1 Corinthians 15:49.
[248] Genesis 1:26-27.

Rendering

The Greek word for "inscription" is "επιγραφ"—"epigraph." This word, "epigraph," is used only here and one other place in the New Testament. In that other place, the word is used of another Ruler's title, one inscribed on a cross. "King of the Jews" was the "epigraph" above the head of Jesus at Calvary: King of God's Chosen People. And as it has turned out, the message is the same: "Wherever the Cross goes, I rule."

Tiberius Caesar stamped his image on a coin and wrote his title across it. "Therefore," says Jesus, "it's Caesar's. Let him have it. Render his stuff to him."

But Jesus Christ impresses His image on our souls and, with the Cross, writes His title, "Savior and Lord," on our lives. We are God's property! "Therefore," Jesus says, "because of the image and inscription that you bear, render yourselves to God."

Submit yourselves to Him as is His due.

❧

"Okay, but how do you 'render' yourself to the God 'from Whom all blessings flow'?"[249]

As the hymn says, "We give [Him] but [His] own, whate'er the gift may be...."[250] In the traditional wedding ceremony, a man and a woman give each other a gold ring as a token of their love for, and commitment to, each other. They say, "...with all that I am and all that I have, I honor you."[251]

How do you render to God what is God's?

Everything you are and everything you have is God's, and with that "everything," you are to honor and worship Him. According to scripture, a portion of who you are and what you have—the first and the best portion—is to be rendered directly to God, dedicated exclusively to God's service.

---

[249] *The Doxology.*
[250] William Walsham How, "We Give Thee But Thine Own," 1858.
[251] From the "Liturgy of Matrimony" in the *Episcopal Book of Common Prayer*, 1928.

From Matthew 22

There is a term for that as well. It is a difficult word to pronounce, but it sounds something like "tithe." And as for the rest, all of who you are and what you have is to be acquired, managed, and expended in a spirit that recognizes and demonstrates your submission to God's sovereignty over you and what you possess. The term for this is "Christian stewardship."

☙❧

So now the cat is out of the bag. All this talk about "rendering to God" is a stewardship sermon.

"People are losing money hand over fist in the stock market and the preacher is talking about giving money to the church."[252]

No, I'm talking—and Jesus is talking—about "rendering," something very different from "giving." Give what you want to—*if* you want to—according to your own sense of gratitude or spirit of generosity. But render to God what as God's, just as you render to the powers of this world what is their due.

"If I do that, I won't be able to take care of myself and my family."

Will God be able to? Has the disaster on Wall Street overwhelmed God the way it has the great companies we once had so much confidence in? Has His power evaporated like the value of so many portfolios? "Be not dismayed whate'er betide, God will take care of you."[253]

"If I render to God like you're talking about, I won't be able to maintain my standard of living."

That may be true, but do you think that God will not be able to maintain His standard for your life? Do you think you will have to do without anything God wants you to have?

Do not be too concerned about the dramatic events of late. Jesus says the benefits of prosperity can become barriers to

---

[252] This sermon was preached in late 2008, at the beginning of the economic downturn.
[253] Civilla D. Martin, "God Will Take Care of You," 1904.

Rendering

spiritual growth and maturity. If you have less of the things of this world, will you not have more room for the things of God? The absence or reduction of material things can bring about a reordering of perspective and agenda that looks more properly to God as the true foundation and focus of life.

Isn't it interesting that Jesus would tell us to render things we think we need to a God Who, we know, doesn't need them at all. We always want to render less to (our current version of) "Caesar," no matter how patriotic we are. Why shouldn't we render less to God, especially in these difficult and uncertain times? God doesn't need our stuff; why does He require that we render it?

Perhaps, among other things, God wants us to know the joy, excitement, pride and satisfaction of participating in His work.[254] Perhaps He wants to give us the opportunity to determine some of how His purpose will be worked out in the world.[255] After all, things happen as a result of our stewardship. They don't happen in its absence. Perhaps the sacrificial stewardship of our time, talents, and treasure, rendered to God, stamps His image more clearly upon us, and inscribes His name and title more thoroughly across our lives, and makes us more completely His, than any other action we could take. Whatever the reason, we are responsible to God for rendering to God the things that are God's.

The question was about money. The issue—still—is the will of God.

---

[254] 2 Corinthians 8:1-4.
[255] Matthew 25:14-29.

26.

The Teacher's Take on Taxes

Matthew 22:15-22 NRSV (p. 180)

It was a Monday. The day before, Jesus had entered Jerusalem—triumphantly, by all accounts—surrounded by Passover pilgrims singing His praises:

"Jesus, the prophet!"

"Jesus, the Son of David!"

"Jesus, the Messiah?"

As they snaked their way through the narrow city streets, the crowd swelled and swarms of little street urchins joined the procession, drawn, as they always are, by anything out of the ordinary. The parade of people escorted Jesus right into the temple where the religious establishment was getting ready for the Passover extravaganza coming up.

To accommodate the crush of out-of-towners who always showed up for the big holiday, the temple leaders had set up a temporary ATM system for currency exchange, and sacrifice supporting mini-marts, in convenient locations inside the temple complex.

Jesus the Pilgrim was impressed—but not in an appreciative way. The crowd was still chanting "Hosanna!" when Jesus turned into a one-man wrecking crew, turning over tables and scattering mounds of money and a menagerie of animals—and the men who were making a profit on both. Chaos reigned in the corridors of the temple.

By the time word got up to the executive offices and the chief priests rushed down (with their lawyers in tow) to witness the mayhem, Jesus had moved on to the pathetic pilgrims clumped around the temple—people who had brought their pain and hopes to God. Rage turned to compassion as Jesus touched the blind and made them see. He touched the lame and made them walk.

And then another glorious, joyous kind of chaos broke out: "*That's* what you ought to be doing in the House of God!" The kids started yelling "Hosanna!" again, and the temple staff's carefully conceived marketing plan for Passover was in shambles.

Shaken to the core, the priests tried to restore some sense of order, pushing their way through the crowd to Jesus and demanding, "Will somebody shut those brats up?!"

"Not if God set them off," Jesus replied. And the temple big shots were savvy enough to sense that everybody seemed to be on the side of this upstart from Galilee. And He certainly wasn't intimidated by their fancy robes or imposing reputations.

In fact, Jesus turned up in their temple, turned it upside down right under their noses, and then left without a "by your leave." Jesus left, but they knew He would come back. And when He did, they would be ready for Him—or so they thought.

❧

Sure enough, Monday morning finds Jesus back in the temple, at the center of an ever-widening circle of people hanging on His every word. And here come the chief priests, with elders of the Jewish ruling council for back up. And like a bunch of religious Barney Fifes, they are determined to "nip this in the bud."

"*By what authority are you doing these things?* Show us your permit to preach and perform miracles. Don't have one, do you?" they say with smug satisfaction.

From Matthew 22

And Jesus replies unfazed, "I got My permit the same place John the Baptist got his. Was John's permit valid?"

Isn't it fascinating how quickly smug satisfaction can morph into something else entirely?

Jesus waits patiently for their answer, and everybody else seems very interested in what they have to say on the subject as well. And yet, all of a sudden, none of the temple leaders feels very much like talking.

So Jesus breaks the silence and poses another question to them: "Suppose a father tells two sons to do some chores and one of them says he will, but doesn't, while the other does his chores, even though he told his dad he wouldn't. Which one is going to be on the father's good side? And guess which one you guys are?"[256]

And while they'll steaming over that little bit of condemnation, Jesus fire off another round: "You guys are like a bunch of hired hands who went berserk in your boss' vineyard.[257] God's going to toss you out and get somebody else in here to do the job right."[258]

You can't spit in the temple, but these guys are mad enough to. And Jesus isn't done with them yet.

"A king invited a bunch of important people to a big party and they snubbed him and attacked his servants. The king wiped them out. Guess who I'm really talking about?"[259]

Well, the chief priests and elders clearly are no match for Jesus, and finally they just march off, sputtering, beating a humiliated retreat to keep Jesus from slamming them again.[260]

But the day is young, and the temple brass aren't the only gang in Jerusalem out to get Jesus. Up in Galilee, Jesus was constantly

---

[256] Matthew 21:28-32.
[257] Matthew 21:33-41.
[258] Matthew 21:43.
[259] Matthew 22:1-7.
[260] Matthew 22:22.

The Teacher's Take on Taxes

being harassed by Pharisees, whose singular claim to fame was taking obedience to the letter of the law to amazing lengths.

Well, it turns out there are Pharisees in Jerusalem, too. And after watching Jesus take the priests apart, the big city Pharisees think somebody has to cut Him down to size—and they're willing to be the ones to do it. But they need a plan. And they are going to need the help of their arch religious enemies, the Herodians.

Herodians are the guys who hang out with Herod. You remember Herod. He's the petty dictator who runs Galilee for the Romans.[261] He's the moral midget who was talked into taking the head of John the Baptist and giving it away as a dance prize.[262] And it's Herod's buddies that the Pharisees decide to make common cause with again Jesus. Can you imagine what it must take to get Pharisees and Herodians both to hate someone else more than they hate each other?

It's incredible, but here they come, Pharisees and Herodians, ready to take Jesus on, ready to spring the trap that cannot fail to bring Him down.

"Look out, Jesus! It's time to play another round of 'Trick Questions.' Your question for today is, 'What is Your take on taxes?'"

❧

Nobody cares about taxes today, of course, but in the time of Jesus, this was a very hot issue. The tax they're talking about is the tax the Romans imposed on the countries they conquered.

The Pharisees—and almost all the Jews—hate the tax they have to pay to Rome. They don't think Jews should have to pay it. They don't think God *wants* them to pay it. They *wouldn't* pay it, if Rome didn't make them—which Rome does, with Herod's help.

---

[261] Josephus, *Antiquities of the Jews*, Book XVIII, Chapter 2, §1.
[262] Matthew 14:1-11.

From Matthew 22

Herod is for the tax. So are his Herodians. They're about the only Jews who are. They're for it because they take their cut off the top before it goes off to Rome—off to Caesar.

So, the Herodians are for taxes; the Pharisees and the rest of the Jews are against them.

"So, how about it, Jesus? Is it right for Jews to pay Caesar's tax? What do You think God wants us to do about this tax?"

Of course, if You say "yes" to the tax, all the Jews will know You're a Roman "toady."

If You say, "No. Don't pay the tax," You'll be in jail—or dead—by nightfall, courtesy of the Romans who take a very dim view of discouraging the payment of the taxes they impose.

And here's the funny thing: The Pharisees and the Herodians don't actually care which side Jesus comes down on. Whoever He agrees with isn't going to support or defend Him. They're going to let their enemies—and His—tear Him apart. That's what makes it such a beautiful plan—such an exquisite trap. "O Teacher! O Rabbi! You're so wise and noble and courageous. We know You'll want to step right into our trap."

And Jesus looks over at the Pharisees looking back at Him with faces fixed in an expression of plastic piety, then across to the Herodians who can't quite keep the cynical sneers out of their oily smiles, and around at the fascinated crowd who can't figure out how He's going to get out of *this* one, though they wish He could, because, truth be told, most Jews don't really like Pharisees *or* Herodians.

And Jesus says, "Yes, that's a mighty fine trap. But before I step into it, why don't one of you show Me one of those Roman coins they make you pay the Roman tax with?"

❧

Now that wasn't part of the plan. And the thing is: no one has one of those coins in his possession—or at least none of them will admit it. There shouldn't be one in the temple, because the particular coin in question has the likeness of Tiberius, the current Caesar, on it. And around the image—the *graven* image—of Caesar, is an inscription that says, "Caesar is the son of the divine Augustus"—the son of a god. Every one of those coins is a violation of the Second Commandment. By rights, an observant Jew should not carry one of those coins; probably should not even look at one.

But they do find one of those coins and bring it to Jesus. Where did they get it? If not from one of the Herodians, they probably got it from the money-changers' tables Jesus turned over the day before.[263] You know the chief priests would have set everything back up just like it was as soon as Jesus left the complex.

You can't pay the other tax—the Jewish temple tax—with a Roman coin, but the temple staff will certainly sell you a temple coin for the price of the Roman one—and a little more.

"Jesus, just step in the trap already!"

But Jesus says, "Whose image? Whose inscription? Whose coin?"

Impatient to get on with it, and not having noticed that their carefully laid trap has been repositioned, they answer Jesus: "Caesar's"

"Then give it to Caesar if it's his. But give God what belongs to Him. Give God what bears His likeness, His image. Give God the things He has marked with His word."

❧

Jesus sidesteps the trap without taking a step. And there are the Pharisees and Herodians, who thought they had a sure thing, only to discover that they are the ones caught in the trap of the trick question.

As it turns out, the Teacher doesn't have a "take" on taxes. He understands that they have asked Him the wrong question, so He

---

[263] Matthew 21:12.

From Matthew 22

just answers the right one, instead: "Sure, if you have to pay taxes, pay them. You don't have a choice; the government's going to make you. Give it to Caesar.

"But that doesn't mean you should have to. A government doesn't have the right to tax just because it's a government. Caesar is not God.

"But that's not the point, either. The point is that whatever Caesar wants from you, *you* belong to God. You bear His image, His likeness. God has written His word in your mind and upon your heart. God created you and everything in your world to be His. And it all remains His, whether you pay it out to Caesar as your civic duty, or hand it out in charity to someone in need, or hold it in trust for God's service."

Caesar can take things from you. If he does, don't worry; God will supply all your needs.[264]

But God wants things from you as well. He does not tax you; He does not need anything He has given you. But God does want you to give Him what is His when He asks it.

Why He asks is His business. We can only guess why, based on what we know of Him, based on our experience of that part of Himself He has placed upon us and within us.[265]

"Why?" really doesn't matter. What matters is that we are to give Him what is His.

The Teacher came into the temple and turned everything upside down. If what He said about "what we are to give to whom" is right, He has turned everything about *our* world upside down as well.

ঔ∾ঌ

---

[264] Philippians 4:19.
[265] Genesis 1:27; Ephesians 3:14-19.

The Greatest Commandment

Matthew 22:34-40 NRSV

³⁴ When the Pharisees heard that [Jesus] had silenced the Sadducees, they gathered together, ³⁵ and one of them, a lawyer, asked him a question to test him. ³⁶ "Teacher, which commandment in the law is the greatest?" ³⁷ He said to him, "'You shall love the Lord your God with all your heart, and with all your soul, and with all your mind.' ³⁸ This is the greatest and first commandment. ³⁹ And a second is like it: 'You shall love your neighbor as yourself.' ⁴⁰ On these two commandments hang all the law and the prophets."

27.

The Greatest Commandment

Matthew 22:34-40 NRSV

So, as our liturgy says each week: "Hear what our Lord Jesus Christ saith."[266] Sunday after Sunday, you barely get the hymnal back in the rack and yourself comfortable in your pew before you're told to love God—and your neighbor.

This is "biblical DNA," everything else in the Old Testament is contained within it and grows out of it. It's the proper and appropriate response of every Christian to the salvation God has provided in Jesus Christ: "Lord, I want to be a Christian in my heart—in my heart."[267]

Fine. Love the Lord your God with all your heart. And while you're at it, love Him with all your soul and mind, too. And while you're loving God, love everybody God created and put here on this earth with you.

"But...." No buts. Thou shalt. It's like a commandment—non-negotiable. You got a problem with it, take it up with Jesus, He's the One Who "saith" it.

---

[266] From the beginning of the communion liturgy in the *Episcopal Book of Common Prayer*, 1928.
[267] "Lord, I Want to Be a Christian," an American spiritual from the 1750s.

The Greatest Commandment

"But wait a minute! What does it mean to love God and my 'neighbor'? And how can you 'command' someone to love?"

Last question first. I can't command you to love, but God apparently can. God commands love in the ancient law found in Deuteronomy and Leviticus, the verses Jesus quotes,[268] and in the words of Jesus quoting them.

In other words, don't wait until you feel like loving God. Do whatever it is you do when you love someone. Pay attention to Him. Spend time with Him, in public and when it's just the two of you. Sing His praises, to Him and to anyone who will listen. Do what He wants you to do.

Just as your feelings demand that you do these things when you love someone, God demands that you love Him, but not just with your feelings. God demands that you stir up the emotions in your heart so that you feel a holy and appropriately grateful love for the God Who has loved you first[269] and far better than you could ever love Him.[270]

God demands that you direct the thoughts in your mind to what He has done for you so that the intellectual awareness of God's love drives you to an amazed appreciation of His unexpected and unmerited love for you.[271]

God demands that you recognize that you, as the particular person you are—your unique identity—is a gift from God—that the reason your very soul exists is to know God in an eternal relationship of love…[272]

❧❦

…which is also true for the soul of every other person conceived in God's ongoing Creation.

---

[268] Deuteronomy 6:5; Leviticus 19:34.
[269] 1 John 4:19.
[270] Ephesians 5:2.
[271] Ephesians 2:4-7.
[272] Psalm 139:13-18.

From Matthew 22

Mr. Jefferson got it right (if we make allowance for the literary conventions of his time) when he wrote that "all men are created equal and are endowed by their Creator...."[273] We are all the products of God's creative love and the subjects of His sustaining love. You love God? Love everybody God loves.

"Love them!? I don't even like most of them!"

You are not required to like your neighbor. He or she may not be very likable at all.

But remember, there are times when God doesn't like you, or at least the things you're doing, which, practically speaking, are the indication of who you are at the time you're doing them.

But God always loves you. And He loves your neighbors, near and far, wherever they come down on the "likeability spectrum."

If you love God as directed—with everything you've got—the relationship that will develop with Him will generate the ability to love those frequently unlikable humans designated by Jesus Christ as your neighbors.

Loving God will enable you to love your neighbor. Loving your neighbor will demonstrate that you love God. In both cases, the love God commands brings about ever deepening, ever maturing relationships with God and man that fulfill the last and least obvious love requirement contained in these greatest commandments: loving yourself.

☙❧

The way God wants you to love other people is the way God wants you to love yourself.

We generally care more about ourselves than about anybody else, which is why God pegs our required interest in others to our typical, selfish interest in ourselves. But God does not desire that your love for Him or others be selfish or petty, fawning or

---

[273] Thomas Jefferson, *The Declaration of Independence*, July 4, 1776.

The Greatest Commandment

indulgent. And so, your love for yourself cannot be that way, either.

Obeying the Great Commandment paves the way for your relationship with God to be pleasing to God and fulfilling to you. Loving your neighbor because you love God will enable you to love neighbors—those often pesky other people—in a mature, responsible way.

Loving God and your neighbors molds the identity, intellect and emotions you have devoted to God so that rather than selfishly indulging yourself in whatever you want, or guiltily reproving yourself for all your shortcomings, you can love yourself maturely and productively (in the way God loves you).

Love God fully. Love yourself and others beneficially.

It's all there in these greatest of all commandments.

"Hear what our Lord Jesus Christ saith."

28.

Big Shots, Beware!

Matthew 23:1-12 NRSV

¹ Then Jesus said to the crowds and to his disciples, ² "The scribes and the Pharisees sit on Moses' seat; ³ therefore, do whatever they teach you and follow it; but do not do as they do, for they do not practice what they teach. ⁴ They tie up heavy burdens, hard to bear,¹ and lay them on the shoulders of others; but they themselves are unwilling to lift a finger to move them. ⁵ They do all their deeds to be seen by others; for they make their phylacteries broad and their fringes long. ⁶ They love to have the place of honor at banquets and the best seats in the synagogues, ⁷ and to be greeted with respect in the marketplaces, and to have people call them rabbi. ⁸ But you are not to be called rabbi, for you have one teacher, and you are all students. ⁹ And call no one your father on earth, for you have one Father—the one in heaven. ¹⁰ Nor are you to be called instructors, for you have one instructor, the Messiah.¹ ¹¹ The greatest among you will be your servant. ¹² All who exalt themselves will be humbled, and all who humble themselves will be exalted."

❧

The sermon today is not for everybody. It may be for you; it may not. The sermon today is for the Big Shots who are here: sitting in the pews—and, perhaps, standing in the pulpit. It is important for Big Shots to hear this sermon, because it contains an important warning. But before I deliver the warning, I need to define the recipients. Who are the Big Shots among us?

Jesus was talking about Big Shot religious leaders in the passage from Matthew: scribes and Pharisees, people who spent more time and effort studying the Bible and conforming their lives and behavior to what the Bible said than anybody else.

If that's what a Big Shot is, we're in trouble here, because we *want* you more involved in Bible study and more committed to a biblical lifestyle.

Fortunately, Jesus wasn't criticizing dedication to the Word of God or the Christian life. The problem with these leaders was not that they were Bible teachers, but that they had decided to become Big Shots in the process.

How did they become Big Shots? They did not practice what they preached (or taught). They did all their deeds to be seen by others. They loved the places of honor, the best seats, to be greeted with respect and treated—well—like Big Shots.

They were not Big Shots because they were important people or because what they did was important. They were Big Shots because they wanted to be Big Shots—because they saw themselves as Big Shots, and acted like Big Shots, like they were as important as, or more important than, the important work they were doing.

And that's how we become Big Shots. We exalt ourselves. We raise ourselves in our own estimation above the level or place we should occupy.

And we may have help.

If people assure us that we should occupy the exalted positions we desire—if they applaud what we do for them to see—if they insist we take the places of honor we crave, it's a whole lot easier to raise ourselves in our own estimation. We shine and everything else fades. We become Big Shots.

But look out! Something significant always happens to Big Shots. Jesus says those who exalt themselves—those who choose

From Matthew 23

to become Big Shots in their own estimation—will be humbled. Inevitably, those who put themselves on a pedestal will be toppled off it. I know this to be true from personal experience:

At the first men's breakfast I attended after you called me here, they asked me how I wanted to be addressed. I responded that my preference was to be called "Your Majesty." I suppose, in retrospect, I was exalting myself a little. They certainly wasted no time in humbling me—"big time."

Why do we want to be Big Shots? It's a temptation as old as Adam and Eve, and as current as Tuesday's election. We are not content to be the crown of God's Creation.[274] We want to be more. We want to be like God[275] and so we pretend that *our* wisdom and *our* power and *our* purposes are like His. We do not want to trust in God's wisdom.[276] We do not want to depend on God's power. We do not want to accept His purpose, for us and all of His Creation.

All this, ironically, is because we do not realize how important we really are to God. The world tells us we are only as important as our productivity. They tell us our value is tied to our physical beauty or our bank balance, to our ability to manage or motivate. We want to be important, but we frequently fear or feel that we are not. We decide to make up a deficit that is not there—and end up creating one in the process.

So Big Shots, beware! Self-exaltation is counter-productive. It merely intensifies the humbling that will surely come. Isaac Newton said that, in physics, every action produces an equal and opposite reaction.[277] It holds pretty true for human relations as well. Whatever you do, somebody will sooner or later come along to oppose it. The bigger your effort—the stronger the opposition.

---

[274] Genesis 1:26-28.
[275] Genesis 3:1-6.
[276] Proverbs 3:5.
[277] Isaac Newton, "Newton's Third Law of Motion," *Mathematical Principles of Natural Philosophy*, 1687.

Big Shots, Beware!

Puff yourself up, and somebody will become obsessed with popping your bubble.

It's the "pecking order" thing. We create pecking orders all the time. Watch kids on a playground or in a schoolroom. They know there is a pecking order and where they fit into it. Some fiercely defend their place at the top and others are struggling to get up there. These are the Big Shots.

But eventually, some will be pushed down by those above or around them while others will simply slip and fall, especially when those at the bottom finally decide to step away and stop supporting the weight of those who climbed over them. Those who exalt themselves will be humbled—by life—by other people—and by God Himself.

We are humbled by God, ultimately, because exalting ourselves usurps God's divine prerogative to exalt (and to abase), to raise up and bring down.[278] It is not that God does not want people exalted; it is rather that God wants us exalted in His way—for His purpose. To become a Big Shot—to compete with God over the meaning and purpose for your life—is to set the stage for a great and certain humbling.

So, there's the warning to any Big Shots here today: Beware! Exalt yourself and you will be humbled. That's the way the world works, and more importantly, that's the way God works.

But along with the warning is a promise: "Whoever humbles himself," Jesus says, "will be exalted."

God humbles us, if we have exalted ourselves, in order to make our relationship with Him what it needs to be. If we save Him the trouble and humble ourselves, rejecting the temptation to become Big Shots in our own minds, God will exalt us.

How does God exalt us? Through service: *"the greatest among you will be your servant."*[279] God's idea of greatness is not the honors you receive, but the service you render. (There's that word "render"

---

[278] Psalm 18:27.
[279] Matthew 23:11.

again.) Jesus set the example of greatness Himself. If anybody had a right to be a Big Shot, to exalt Himself, it was Jesus. But He exalted servanthood instead. As God's servant, Jesus served those God wanted served, and in so doing, achieved true greatness.

Jesus was a servant, but He wasn't servile.[280] What He was, was intentionally and thoroughly humble—before God.[281] God had given Him great ability. And with humility, Jesus exercised that ability to achieve great things.[282]

If you humble yourself before God, He will exalt you to the role of servant, the lofty spiritual position of those who accomplish great things in and for God's kingdom. In a few minutes, we will pray the Prayer of Humble Access and tell God, "We are not worthy."[283] It's another way of saying, "Lord, I'm no Big Shot. You don't have to humble me."

And after we share in Communion, we will give thanks to God for feeding us and assuring us of His favor and goodness, signs that He has exalted us for His service. It's our way of saying "Thanks for exalting me."

So, let's review.

The warning is severe: "Exalt yourself and God will bring you down. God will allow no Big Shots in His kingdom!"

But the promise is sublime: "Humble yourself and God will lift you up and make you bigger than any Big Shot could ever imagine."

Halleluiah for the promise!

But Big Shots, be warned—and beware.

❧

---

[280] John 13:1-14.
[281] Matthew 11:29.
[282] John 5:19-20.
[283] From the Communion Liturgy in the *Episcopal Book of Common Prayer*, 1928.

A Lesson in Leadership

1 Thessalonians 2:9-13 ESV

⁹ For you remember, brothers, our labor and toil: we worked night and day, that we might not be a burden to any of you, while we proclaimed to you the gospel of God. ¹⁰ You are witnesses, and God also, how holy and righteous and blameless was our conduct toward you believers. ¹¹ For you know how, like a father with his children, ¹² we exhorted each one of you and encouraged you and charged you to walk in a manner worthy of God, who calls you into his own kingdom and glory.

¹³ And we also thank God constantly for this, that when you received the word of God, which you heard from us, you accepted it not as the word of men but as what it really is, the word of God, which is at work in you believers.

Matthew 23:1-12 ESV

¹ Then Jesus said to the crowds and to his disciples, ² "The scribes and the Pharisees sit on Moses' seat, ³ so do and observe whatever they tell you, but not the works they do. For they preach, but do not practice. ⁴ They tie up heavy burdens, hard to bear, and lay them on people's shoulders, but they themselves are not willing to move them with their finger. ⁵ They do all their deeds to be seen by others. For they make their phylacteries broad and their fringes long, ⁶ and they love the place of honor at feasts and the best seats in the synagogues ⁷ and greetings in the marketplaces and being called rabbi by others. ⁸ But you are not to be called rabbi, for you have one teacher, and you are all brothers. ⁹ And call no man your father on earth, for you have one Father, who is in heaven. ¹⁰ Neither be called instructors, for you have one instructor, the Christ. ¹¹ The greatest among you shall be your servant. ¹² Whoever exalts himself will be humbled, and whoever humbles himself will be exalted."

29.

A Lesson in Leadership

1 Thessalonians 2:9-13; Matthew 23:1-12 ESV

If you go browsing in a bookstore, somewhere in the non-fiction area you will find a section on "Leadership." In a small store, it may only be a shelf. In a large store, you may be confronted with an entire aisle on the subject, with dozens and dozens of books offering up the insights and advice of business, industry and government giants.

What you probably won't find in the leadership section, but should, is the Bible. Nowhere is there deeper insight or better advice on leadership than that found in the pages of scripture—as we shall see today.

Lessons in leadership would not be important for most of us, except for one thing: we are Christians, and every Christian is called to be a leader.[284] Your Leader, Christ, has made it very clear that everyone who follows Him—every Christian—is to be leading others. You are to be leading people to Christ. You are to be leading people into His Church. You are to be leading your fellow Christians, as Paul put it in the epistle reading today, "to live lives worthy of God."

---

[284] Matthew 28:19-20.

We ask you to wear a name tag every Sunday. (Some who have special responsibilities in the service wear more than one.)

We could write "Christian Leader" under every name and we wouldn't be wrong—if you are a Christian. Christ, our Leader, has appointed every one of us—every disciple—to a position of leadership in the Church.

❦

"But I'm not a leader!"

You are if He says you are. You have been appointed a leader by Jesus Himself—and what is more—He has equipped you for the job: He has given you the Holy Spirit to empower you. What you lack in gifts and abilities, energy and experience, the Holy Spirit makes up.

You have been given the Bible, containing more practical insight and advice about leadership than all the other books ever written on the subject combined. In the Bible, the giants of the faith instruct you in leadership: Moses and Joshua, David and Daniel, Ezra and Nehemiah, Peter and Paul and Jesus Himself.

Look! Your Leader has made you a leader and He has equipped you for the job. You can lead, and Christ expects you to.

Of course, there is a difference between being a leader and being "in charge." In my time in the military, I observed many young men and women who wanted desperately to be "in charge" so they could lead. It generally worked the other way around. Those who demonstrated they could lead were eventually put in charge.

The truth is that you can be a superb leader and not be in charge of anything. To be called and equipped to lead as a Christian does not mean that you are necessarily called or equipped to be in charge, whether of a denomination, church, class or committee. It does mean that wherever you are in this fellowship, with whatever gifts you do have,[285] you are to exercise leadership in the Body of Christ to further the work of His kingdom.[286]

In recent months, the political class in this country has been yammering over whether somebody who is in charge should forego the authority of that position to "lead from behind."

They'll never settle that one. And for most of us, that's a non-issue because most people will almost always be leading from behind or, at best, from beside. That's where we are. And leaders lead from where they are.

But *how* are you to lead as a Christian?

☙❧

Time for a lesson in leadership.

There are actually two lessons today: one from Jesus and one from Paul. Both offer examples, and Christians are to lead, in part at least, by example.

The example Jesus presents is negative on the whole: "Look at this," He says to His disciples. "Look, but do not copy." Leadership, according to Jesus, requires both preaching and practicing. This doesn't mean that you need to sign up to give the sermon one Sunday. But it does mean that Christian leadership—your leadership as a Christian—is not to be only about behavior. There are things you are to say, as well as things you are to do, if you are to be the leader Christ intends for you to be.

Christ shared some insight and advice about leadership when He criticized the religious leaders of His day. He wasn't after them for what they were saying, but for *not* doing what they were telling other people to do. And, to be fair, He also noted that they *were*, in some cases, doing things godly leaders should *not* be doing, regardless of what they were saying. They were certainly in charge, but they were not leading properly.

---

[285] Romans 12:6-8.
[286] Ephesians 4:11-13.

To summarize the critique Jesus offered:
- Practice what you preach.
- Don't make it harder on people to be obedient to God than it has to be.
- Don't show off.
- Don't cultivate a personal fan club.
- Lead with genuine humility.

For Jesus, true leadership—both His leadership and the leadership He requires of His followers—is servant leadership: *"The greatest among you will be your servant."*

And He was.

Jesus was, by far, the greatest among us. He fed the multitudes[287] and calmed the seas[288] and healed the sick.[289] But He also strapped on a towel to wash dirty feet[290] and then strapped on a cross to wash away our sins;[291] He did the work of the ultimate Servant. And because He was *our* Servant, amazing as that is, we, too, are to be servants—servants leading.

But how? How are you to be the leader Christ has called and equipped you to be?

How do you do it?

The answer is: "Preach and practice—practice and preach."

Paul reminded the Christians in Thessalonica what he and others had said and done as their leaders. "Remember, we came alongside you and led you from there. We did not make it harder for you to be Christians; we did not lord our leadership over you. We shared the Christian life with you.

---

[287] John 6:1-13.
[288] Mark 4:35-39.
[289] Matthew 4:24.
[290] John 13:2-5.
[291] Titus 3:3-7.

From Matthew 23

"What did we do? We took care of ourselves as best we could. We lived with you and showed you, in our behavior, holy, righteous and blameless lives. We practiced our faith so openly, consistently and committedly, that you never had to wonder if we really meant what we said to you about the gospel of Jesus Christ. You saw the truth in our lives every time you saw us."

That's what Christian leaders do to lead. When you live your life in holiness and righteousness, leaving no opportunity for anyone to challenge your dedication to Christ and His gospel, you have positioned yourself to be the effective Christian leader Christ has called you to be.

And once you have established the practice of Christianity as your way of life, you are ready to "preach" the gospel persuasively, whatever words you use.

And how did Paul preach to his fellow Christians?

He spoke encouragement to them. He spoke comfort. And he challenged them like a father with his beloved children to grow up in the faith and behave themselves in ways that bring honor and glory to God. Paul modeled his leadership on the leadership of Jesus, so that those he led to Jesus could do the same.

In this congregation, there are encouragers. Sitting among us today are holy comforters.

You are disciples of Jesus Christ who have given your lives to Him and then received them back from Him, filled with His Spirit and guided by His Word, in order that you might be the leaders of the community of faith He has called you to be, transforming lives in and beyond this fellowship, not by your own abilities, but by the miraculous gifts of God given to you as the equipment of leadership.

Every Christian—every one of you—is a leader in the Kingdom of God. Every one of you is called and equipped to be the servant of salvation, leading those around you by your life and your testimony, loving those you lead like Christ loves them—and you.

A Lesson in Leadership

This fellowship does not exist because preachers were willing to preach for you. It has not flourished because of the commitment and expertise of a few talented and dedicated souls. It will not become what God intends for it to be merely by the work and prayers of those in charge.

Every one of you has led this church forward. Every one of you is leading by word and deed, large or small. Every one of you is called to lead. Every one of you is equipped to lead. Every one of you as a Christian is a leader. God has seen to that.

You lead your leaders by your encouragement. You lead those who are burdened with your comfort. You lead the tempted by your dedication to holy and righteous living. You lead the cynical and doubting by your blameless example and unshakable hope. You lead the tired and dispirited, if there are any, by your confidence and enthusiasm—in and for Christ, first—and because of that, in and for this fellowship.

Whether here and now, or somewhere else during the week, your every word—your every deed—is leadership—Christian leadership—Christ using you to move His Church in the direction He intends to take it.

Who's the leader? If you're looking up here or around the room, don't bother. Look in the mirror.

It's you!

Matthew 25:14-30 NRSV

[Jesus said:]

14 "For it is as if a man, going on a journey, summoned his slaves and entrusted his property to them; 15 to one he gave five talents, to another two, to another one, to each according to his ability. Then he went away.

16 "The one who had received the five talents went off at once and traded with them, and made five more talents. 17 In the same way, the one who had the two talents made two more talents.

18 "But the one who had received the one talent went off and dug a hole in the ground and hid his master's money.

19 "After a long time the master of those slaves came and settled accounts with them. 20 Then the one who had received the five talents came forward, bringing five more talents, saying, 'Master, you handed over to me five talents; see, I have made five more talents.' 21 His master said to him, 'Well done, good and trustworthy slave; you have been trustworthy in a few things, I will put you in charge of many things; enter into the joy of your master.'

22 "And the one with the two talents also came forward, saying, 'Master, you handed over to me two talents; see, I have made two more talents.' 23 His master said to him, 'Well done, good and trustworthy slave; you have been trustworthy in a few things, I will put you in charge of many things; enter into the joy of your master.'

24 "Then the one who had received the one talent also came forward, saying, 'Master, I knew that you were a harsh man, reaping where you did not sow, and gathering where you did not scatter seed; 25 so I was afraid, and I went and hid your talent in the ground. Here you have what is yours.'

26 "But his master replied, 'You wicked and lazy slave! You knew, did you, that I reap where I did not sow, and gather where I did not scatter? 27 Then you ought to have invested my money with the bankers, and on my return I would have received what was my own with interest. 28 So take the talent from him, and give it to the one with the ten talents.'

29 "'For to all those who have, more will be given, and they will have an abundance; but from those who have nothing, even what they have will be taken away.

Required to Risk

[30] *"'As for this worthless slave, throw him into the outer darkness, where there will be weeping and gnashing of teeth.'"*

30.

Required to Risk

Matthew 25:14-30 NRSV

These days,[292] digging a hole in the ground and burying your money sounds like a pretty astute investment strategy. You could pretty much count on it being there when you went to dig it up later.

But before you go looking for a shovel, you might want to think about what Jesus had to say on the subject. Jesus has a different perspective about the business of money management.

Jesus told a story about a man who gave his money to people who worked for him. And then the man took off. We'll talk about that man in a minute, but first, let's talk about his money. We're talking about some "serious money" here, as my daddy used to say.

When they talk about "talents" in the Bible, they're not talking skills or abilities like we do. They're talking about money—cold, hard cash. A talent was a measurement, a weight. It was the heaviest weight category they had. When this guy in the story is dropping talents on his servants, we're talking tons of money. Five talents? Think: armored truck. Two talents? Maybe a forklift. One talent? That's a wheelbarrow full of money, at the very least.

---

[292] This sermon was preached at the beginning of the economic downturn in 2008-2009.

These guys are weighed down with money—and with responsibility. You see, these are not Christmas bonuses or tax refunds. It's not quarterly dividends or lottery winnings. It's venture capital.

The owner of the money has entrusted what belongs to him to them—for a purpose. He gives them his valuable assets, but with significant strings attached. They're rolling in dough, but he expects there to be a lot more of it when he comes back.

It's a heavy responsibility. But if the responsibility is so heavy, why don't they just turn the man down? Why don't they walk away from the deal?

They probably can't.

The Greek word used to describe these guys means "servants"—or "slaves." You wouldn't think a slave could be a big-time money manager, but many were in the time of Jesus. Your ability determined your type and level of work, whatever your status as slave or free. The man owned the money he gave them, and he probably owned them, too, if he had the authority to do with them what he ordered at the end.

The man had purchased them, and he provided for them, but he also had the right to assign them tasks in his service. What he gave them to do was to take his money and use it to make more of it. They were required to make a profit with the fortunes he supplied them. And don't think they didn't know it. They knew him, and they knew what he expected.

He also knew them. He knew what each was capable of doing. He gave them resources and responsibilities according to their individual abilities, some more—some less. But he wanted them all to succeed in their assignments and he equipped them all for success.

Then this owner of men and money went on his way.

Two of his people went to work immediately with what he had given them—as he intended. But a third went away and buried the treasure his master had given him. This last fellow's conservative strategy ensured the preservation of the principal—and the impossibility of attaining any profit with it.

He also ensured his own condemnation from the owner of the assets who required all his people to take risks with his resources in order to increase them. The master didn't want the money, he wanted what the money could do—the profit that would be realized when a good and faithful servant devoted all his abilities to putting its power to work for the master's purpose.

❧

In the Navy, a sailor may be required to stand before his commanding officer as a result of his performance. It's called "going to mast" because in the days of sailing ships, the captain would be standing in front of a mast when the sailor reported to him.

There are two kinds of mast. One is "Meritorious Mast," in which someone is recognized and commended for especially effective service. The officer in charge praises the individual for his superior achievement and may pin a medal on him or promote him on the spot. It is a great thing to have a meritorious mast.

On the other hand, there is what is simply called, "Captain's Mast," where one who has disobeyed orders and preformed very poorly is required to give account of himself. The captain will listen to any defense the individual standing at attention before him may choose to offer, but the outcome is seldom in question because the sailor's guilt is already known.

The captain will dismantle the sailor's excuses and declare judgment upon him. Punishment will be imposed. His rank, his pay, and his freedom may be taken away from him. He may even be thrown out of the Navy—losing all the benefits he enjoyed in the service. No sailor wants to be taken to Captain's Mast.

When the man in the Bible came back from his journey, he "held mast" on those he had entrusted with his property. Two went to meritorious mast: "Well done, good and faithful servants. I will appoint you over many things. Share my joy."

The third man suffered a different fate. Oh, he got to offer his defense: "You're hard and have high expectations," he told his master, "and I was afraid of what you would do if I failed in my assignment, so I didn't even try to carry it out."

His master—and now his judge—is not impressed: "I required you to do your best with what I gave you—and you decided not to do anything with it at all?! Did you expect me to be satisfied when you did not fulfill your assignment—because you disobeyed my orders?! I find you guilty. I order you to forfeit everything and to be cast out of my command!"

In this way, the parable is like the Navy.

❧

But it is also, according to Jesus, like the kingdom of God. You may never have been a sailor, standing before your captain, trying to explain why you didn't do what he commanded you to do. But we will all stand before the One Who has given us great treasures and required us to use those resources to increase His kingdom.

Some were standing before Jesus as He told this story who were not happy about what they were hearing. They were not happy because they were playing it safe with the great things God had given them. They were religious—very religious, but they were also afraid of God.

And so they decided to do nothing spiritually that was risky, to take no chances religiously. Sit tight and preserve the status quo. Protect the word of God. Don't take it out into the rough and tumble world where it might get abused—and might make a profit in transformed lives.

Do you think playing it safe with whatever God has given you will please God? Do you think that's why He has given you everything you have? Are you afraid of God's wrath or of His requirement that you put the treasure He has entrusted to you at

From Matthew 25

risk for the sake of His kingdom? Remember: "The Lord giveth and the Lord taketh away."[293]

He "giveth," not for our pleasure or comfort, but for the profit in people we can bring to His kingdom by expending His resources to save souls and bless lives in His Name. He "taketh away" when we do not invest as He intends—risky as it may seem.

He takes what you will not risk from you so that His abundant material and spiritual resources may be placed in the hands and hearts of those who will go and work with them and realize the increase He desires and demands.

"But these are hard financial times."

And the times of Jesus weren't?!

"Don't expect too much from the pledges this year."

Has God stopped giving His treasure to those who belong to Him, who are willing to risk what God has given to realize a profit for Him?

"We don't need to take on any big projects right now."

Does God prefer that we bury what He has given us, or risk it on great things, things that advance and increase His kingdom?

How are we going to get from where we are to *"Well done, thou good and faithful servant"* if we—the people who are His—do not do—with the resources that are His—what He commanded us to do with them when He gave them?

Who would have thought that the good and faithful servant would be the one who takes what God gives and then takes chances with it? Who would have thought that playing it safe with God's gifts would make you liable for such a harsh and heavy punishment?

Usually, when somebody says, "It's not the money; it the principle of the thing," it's the money. In this case, in this parable about serious money, tons of money, it *is* about the money—and the principle, too. It's about everything of value God has given us.

---

[293] Job 1:21.

Required to Risk

It's about talents in the modern sense—and time—as well as treasure. But most of all, it's about the way God works and the remarkable truth that, to please God, you must join Him in His work and let Him take care of you in the process.

If your goal is self-preservation—if you will not use God's resources in the risky, sacrificial way He intends, you will preserve neither yourself nor your honored place with God.

"I didn't do what you wanted me to do, Lord, but I had a reason."

Do you think it will matter?

"I made sure I enjoyed your blessings to the fullest—I just chose not to carry out your orders."

Wanna guess the verdict God will hand down on that one?

Christianity is a risky business—always has been. But make no mistake: When you risk whatever it may be in the service of the King, there is no risk of displeasing Him.

Praise, promotion and proximity—these are the rewards awaiting the faithful servant when the master returns. Skip the shovel and put what God has given you to work for Him.

From Matthew 25

Matthew 25:31-46 NRSV

[Jesus said:]

³¹ "When the Son of Man comes in his glory, and all the angels with him, then he will sit on the throne of his glory. ³² All the nations will be gathered before him, and he will separate people one from another as a shepherd separates the sheep from the goats, ³³ and he will put the sheep at his right hand and the goats at the left.

³⁴ "Then the king will say to those at his right hand, 'Come, you that are blessed by my Father, inherit the kingdom prepared for you from the foundation of the world; ³⁵ for I was hungry and you gave me food, I was thirsty and you gave me something to drink, I was a stranger and you welcomed me, ³⁶ I was naked and you gave me clothing, I was sick and you took care of me, I was in prison and you visited me.'

³⁷ "Then the righteous will answer him, 'Lord, when was it that we saw you hungry and gave you food, or thirsty and gave you something to drink? ³⁸ And when was it that we saw you a stranger and welcomed you, or naked and gave you clothing? ³⁹ And when was it that we saw you sick or in prison and visited you?'

⁴⁰ "And the king will answer them, 'Truly I tell you, just as you did it to one of the least of these who are members of my family, you did it to me.'

⁴¹ "Then he will say to those at his left hand, 'You that are accursed, depart from me into the eternal fire prepared for the devil and his angels; ⁴² for I was hungry and you gave me no food, I was thirsty and you gave me nothing to drink, ⁴³ I was a stranger and you did not welcome me, naked and you did not give me clothing, sick and in prison and you did not visit me.'

⁴⁴ "Then they also will answer, 'Lord, when was it that we saw you hungry or thirsty or a stranger or naked or sick or in prison, and did not take care of you?'

⁴⁵ "Then he will answer them, 'Truly I tell you, just as you did not do it to one of the least of these, you did not do it to me.'

⁴⁶ "And these will go away into eternal punishment, but the righteous into eternal life."

31.

What a Surprise!

Matthew 25:31-46 NRSV

It's Judgment Day, and everybody is surprised—everybody except Jesus.

Some are no doubt surprised that Jesus is doing the judging. It was always the other way around. Pharisees, chief priests, elders—these guys judged Him unacceptable from the beginning.[294] Pontius Pilate, the Roman governor of Judea, was gradually but effectively maneuvered into passing his own legal—and lethal—judgment on Jesus.[295]

Skeptics across the centuries have lined up behind these early judges to pass their own sentence on Jesus, and to impose it with all the smug superiority and cynical spirit they can muster. In our own day, those determined to judge Jesus invariably find Him "wanting," certain that their criticisms are unarguable and His flaws—in actions and ideas—are both flagrant and fatal.

Of course, they conveniently confuse the shortcomings of the followers of Jesus with the Savior Himself. Everything a Christian does wrong is laid at the feet of Jesus, or across His shoulders, as though He were the whipping boy for the sins, whether real or

---

[294] Matthew 12:14; Matthew 26:3-4.
[295] John 18:28—19:16.

What a Surprise!

imagined, of every believer, as He once was for all the sins of all humanity.[296] Imagine the surprise of all His judges when Jesus turns up on Judgment Day and does some major league judging of His own.[297]

Everyone is surprised, the condemned and the vindicated alike. And there are some at Judgment Day who *are* vindicated—who come out pretty well, according to Matthew.

But all are amazed at the basis for judgment and that the individual cases are judged as they are. Many, no doubt, are surprised that there is a final cosmic Judgment at all. They had convinced themselves that this Judgment business was a logical and scientific impossibility, an outdated superstition.

They now realize they should have kept a more open mind on the subject and even prepared for unanticipated spiritual eventualities. Too late for that now, of course.

Another surprise is that the Judgment produces a dividing. Many people had become convinced that if there were a final exam, no one would be allowed to fail. The grades would be "scaled." Everybody would get promoted—some on merit, the rest out of the goodness of His (the Judge's) heart. Nobody—at least nobody we knew—really had anything to worry about.

That someone would have been found to have failed seemed inconceivable. And yet, it appears, when Jesus hands out the final grades, not everybody passes. There's a lot more drama in this graduation ceremony, and a lot less horsing around, than people have become accustomed to.

Both those who pass and those who fail seem surprised at the way the grades have come out.

Those who pass are surprised they have done well enough to pass, and those who fail don't understand how they have lost so many points. Everybody seems to have forgotten to ask the most essential question of the Teacher now turned Grader: "Will that be

---

[296] Hebrews 7:27.
[297] Matthew 24:29-31.

on the test?" If they did ask, they certainly lost track of the answer He would have given.

Everybody has been graded on recognizing Jesus and treating Him appropriately. The catch is He didn't always look like Himself. Most people never saw Him at all, they just saw the people He was with. The people who came out all right treated the people Jesus was with the way they would treat Jesus if they could see Him—and so they treated Him like they were supposed to without even knowing it.

In the end, they passed the test without knowing it—which is a pretty good thing. How good? *"Come, you that are blessed by My Father, inherit the kingdom prepared for you from the foundation of the world"* good.

But some people don't see Jesus, and don't believe He's with anybody, and so don't believe there's any point in treating anybody like they would treat Jesus if they knew He were present. And so, being mistreated along with those He promised to be *"with... always, to the end of the age,"*[298] Jesus judges those who have mistreated Him and the people He travels with.

For the folks who have mistreated Jesus, the news and their prospects are not good. Their sense of surprise will be accompanied by shock and despair. After all, hearing *"You that are accursed, depart from me into the eternal fire prepared for the devil and his angels"*—is not exactly: "Have a nice day."

Of course, it's only Judgment Day in the story Jesus tells. We have to wait a little longer for the real thing. Jesus Himself didn't know when it would be,[299] but now that He's explained what the final Judgment consists of, there really shouldn't be any surprises. *"As you did it to one of the least of my brothers or sisters, you did it unto me."*

---

[298] Matthew 28:20, ESV.
[299] Matthew 24:36.

All Authority

Matthew 28:16-20 NRSV

[16] Now the eleven disciples went to Galilee, to the mountain to which Jesus had directed them. [17] When they saw him, they worshiped him; but some doubted. [18] And Jesus came and said to them, "All authority in heaven and on earth has been given to me. [19] Go therefore and make disciples of all nations, baptizing them in the name of the Father and of the Son and of the Holy Spirit, [20] and teaching them to obey everything that I have commanded you. And remember, I am with you always, to the end of the age."

32.

All Authority

Matthew 28:16-20 NRSV

The Gospel of Matthew ends with a Galilean rendezvous. After His Resurrection, Jesus left word for His disciples to meet Him in Galilee. They went as He directed, and they saw Him and worshiped Him. What we remember most about the scene is that Jesus issued His Great Commission: *"Go...and make disciples of all the nations, baptizing them in the name of the Father and of the Son and of the Holy Spirit, teaching them to observe all that I have commanded you...."*

The 11 disciples (12 minus Judas) were obedient, as were the other, mainly unnamed and unknown people who followed Jesus during His earthly ministry. They went and made disciples, baptized and taught, and the Church survived and grew.

That Great Commission is still in force, and so we continue to evangelize and teach new Christians the commands of Christ they are to observe. And in this way, the Church has survived 2,000 years of external opposition and internal strife—and has spread around the world.

❦

But there is more in the closing paragraph of this Gospel than the familiar commission. There is a powerful assertion and

All Authority

reassuring promise. The first thing the risen Christ says to His disciples on this occasion is this: *"All authority in heaven and on earth has been given to Me."* A dozen words.... But consider what this means. The Jesus they had known had been a remarkable man with uncommon wisdom and unique power—and then He was grabbed and killed by "the authorities."

Now, He's standing right there in front of them, alive again—and more: not merely remarkable...not just uncommon...more than unique. His is alive, and *"all authority—in heaven and on earth—has been given—to* [Him]."

The Jewish leaders had authority over the religious ritual in the Jerusalem temple and the religious practices of the Jewish people. The Roman governor had authority over the political and military activities in the province of Judea—and, for all practical purposes, in Galilee as well.

And this seemingly insignificant Jewish man they killed is now alive again and claiming an authority infinitely greater than theirs.

❧

What kind of authority are we talking about?

The supreme authority to govern...the supreme authority to require obedience...the supreme authority to appoint to office... the supreme authority to reward and punish...the authority to create and to destroy. It is an astounding claim, when you realize what the claim is.

At the beginning of His ministry, Jesus was tempted with *"...all the kingdoms of the world and their glory...,"*[300] and He refused the offer. Now He has been given all authority, not just on earth, but in heaven as well.

Jesus Christ is the ultimate authority over both the natural and the supernatural: the world we know—or *think* we know—and the realm that stretches infinitely beyond us.

---

[300] Matthew 4:8, ESV.

"All authority in heaven and on earth...." Think of it. Whose authority is that?

With that kind of authority, you could just speak and whatever you said would happen. You could say, *"Let there be light."*[301] And there would be light. You could say, "Let there be life." And that, too, would be. You could say, *"Forgive them for they know not what they do."* [302] And every sin you ever committed would be wiped off the slate as though it never happened. *"All authority in heaven and on earth..."* is the definition of God's power and authority. And it has been given to Jesus Christ our Lord.

"Gentle Jesus, Meek and Mild"?[303]

Only because He has chosen to be, for our sakes. Otherwise, you're dealing with,

"Immortal, invisible God only wise,
in light inaccessible hid from our eyes."[304]

God raised His Incarnate Son Jesus from the dead, not for some honorable retirement in an out-of-the-way heavenly mansion, but to sit enthroned at God's right hand,[305] interceding for His followers[306] until He comes back to judge the whole world.[307] From that position, the Son came as God in Christ to redeem us.[308] And to that position He has returned, sending the Holy Spirit to continue His fellowship with us as our constant and all-sufficient companion[309] until we are brought into His divine Presence for all eternity.[310]

---

[301] Genesis 1:3, KJV.
[302] Luke 23:34, KJV.
[303] Charles Wesley, "Gentle Jesus, Meek and Mild" (Children's hymn), date of composition unknown.
[304] Walter C. Smith, "Immortal, Invisible, God Only Wise," 1867.
[305] Acts 5:30-31.
[306] Romans 8:34.
[307] 2 Timothy 4:1.
[308] Colossians 1:20.
[309] John 14:16-17.
[310] Revelation 7:9-17.

All Authority

All authority in heaven and on earth is His and with that authority He has commissioned us to make disciples. He issues this commission because, although His authority is universal, it is not universally recognized. And those who reject His authority will challenge you who act upon it.

Proclaim the gospel of Jesus Christ and the world responds: "You don't have the right to judge me!" No, but we do have the right and the responsibility to tell you that you have been judged by the One Who does have the right—and you have been found guilty—and you will be dealt with accordingly if you do not repent and submit to this ultimate authority of the universe, repenting and accepting the pardon He offers.

Denial of His authority does not diminish or destroy it. Denial merely puts the deny-er in opposition to it—and makes him or her subject to that authority without protection or recourse.

But you who have come to the risen Jesus, here as He commanded, will see Him in worship, in word and sacrament, even as the Prophet Isaiah saw the Lord, high and lifted up in the temple of his day.[311] You receive the power His authority conveys as you receive His commission. And you receive something else.

You receive the promise of His continuous and powerful Presence. Just as there is nothing in the universe outside His jurisdiction, so there is no place in the universe where you can be separated from His supportive, protecting Presence.[312]

He is always with you forever.

It's a promise you can trust.

It comes on the highest authority.

---

[311] Isaiah 6:1.
[312] Romans 8:38-39.

Indices

Sermon Titles in Alphabetical Order

Title	Page

A Lesson in Leadership 203
A Lesson in Prayer 47
A Question of Identity 143
All Authority 223

Big Shots, Beware! 197
Bizarre Blessings 39
Build Your House 85

Divine Assignment 109

Free to Bear Good Fruit 77

God's Wellness Plan 31

If Your Brother Sins 153
Inauguration Day 5
It's Not Fair! 173

Just Ask 69
Just Passing Through 95

Listen to Jesus 149
Look Who's Invited to Dinner 103

Rendering 179
Required to Risk 211

Sowing Seeds—Bearing Fruit 121
Step Out! 129

Sermon Titles in Alphabetical Order

Title	Page
Tempted As We Are	13
The Games of Childhood	117
The Greatest Commandment	193
The New Guy in Town	23
The Problem with Prosperity	55
The Teacher's Take on Taxes	185
Unity, Liberty, Charity	161
Vineyard Work and Vineyard Wages	167
Walking with Jesus	137
What a Surprise!	219
Will You Give Them Stones?	61

Sermon Texts in Biblical Order

Text	Title	Page

Joshua
4:1-9 — Will You Give Them Stones? 62

1 Samuel
16:11-13 — Inauguration Day 3

Isaiah
43:1-7 — Just Passing Through 93

Matthew
3:1-3, 13-17 — Inauguration Day 4
3:16-17 — Tempted As We Are 12
4:1-11 — Tempted As We Are 12
4:12-23 — The New Guy in Town 22
4:23-25 — God's Wellness Plan 30
5:1-12 — Bizarre Blessings 37
6:5-15 — A Lesson in Prayer 46
6:24-34 — The Problem with Prosperity 54
7:7-11 — Will You Give Them Stones? 61
7:7-11 — Just Ask 68
7:15-20 — Free to Bear Good Fruit 76
7:24-27 — Build Your House 84
8:23-27 — Just Passing Through 94
9:9-13 — Look Who's Invited to Dinner 102
9:37-38 — Divine Assignment 107
10:1-8, 16 — Divine Assignment 107
11:16-30 — The Games of Childhood 116
13:1-9 — Sowing Seeds—Bearing Fruit 121
14:22-33 — Step Out! 127
14:22-33 — Walking with Jesus 136
16:13-20 — A Question of Identity 142
17:1-9 — Listen to Jesus 148
18:15-20 — If Your Brother Sins 152
18:21-35 — Unity, Liberty, Charity 160
20:1-16 — Vineyard Work and Vineyard Wages ... 166

Sermon Texts in Biblical Order

Text	Title	Page

Matthew (Continued)
20:1-16	It's Not Fair!	166
22:15-22	Rendering	178
22:15-22	The Teacher's Take on Taxes	178
22:34-40	The Greatest Commandment	192
23:1-12	Big Shots, Beware!	197
23:1-12	A Lesson in Leadership	202
25:14-30	Required to Risk	209
25:31-46	What a Surprise!	217
28:16-20	All Authority	222

Romans
14:3-11	Unity, Liberty, Charity	159

Galatians
5:13-25	Free to Bear Good Fruit	75

1 Thessalonians
2:9-13	A Lesson in Leadership	202

Hebrews
12:5-11	Build Your House	83

James
1:2-8	Just Ask	68

Sermons from Matthew in Other Volumes

| Text | Title | Page (in Other Volumes) |

In *Our Evil—God's Good*

Matthew
4:1-11	Honor, Virtue and Self-Control	134
5:21-24	You and Me and God	28

In *Things That Kings Can't Do*

Matthew
3 1-3, 13-17	Inauguration Day	46
4:1-11	God's Food in the Desert	134
7:13-19	Lesser Gods—Easier Ways	4
7:24-27	The Forever House	82
7:24-27	The Wisest Thing You'll Ever Do	188

In *In the Presence of the Lord*

Matthew
8:23-27	When You Think You're Going Under	205
15:10-20	Put the Right Stuff In	151
26:36-42	But If Not	167

In *God's Purpose for Your Faith*

Matthew
7:24-27	Build Your House	157

Sermons from Matthew in Other Volumes

Text	Title	Page (in Other Volumes)

In *Making Peace with Your Father*

Matthew
11:16-19, 25-30	A Little Short of Perfection	52
18:21-35	Unity, Liberty, Charity	134
28:1-10	His Resurrection—and Yours	43

In *The Empty God*

Matthew
7:15-20	Free to Bear Good Fruit	28
23:1-12	A Lesson in Leadership	172

In *O Come, Let God Adore Us*

Matthew
1:18-25	The Christmas Problem	94
1:18-25	Your Part in the Process	103
1:18-25	Christmas Almost Didn't Happen	109
2:1-12	Going a Different Way	241
2:1-12	Journey's End	249
3:1-3	Here He Comes	39
11:2-11	Is Jesus the One?	65

In *Not Exactly What They Expected*

Matthew
21:1-11	Look Who's Here	25
27:22-31	Who *Is* This Guy?	107
27:3-54	This is Jesus	115
28:1-10	Life, If You Will Have It	177
28:1-10	His Resurrection—and Yours	185

Sermon Texts in Lectionary Order

Date	Text	Page

Cycle A

Baptism of the Lord	Matthew 3:1-3, 13-17	4
Epiphany 3 [3]	Matthew 4:12-23	22
Epiphany 4 [4]	Matthew 5:1-12	37
Epiphany 8 [8]	Matthew 6:24-34	54
Epiphany 9 [9]	Matthew 7:24-27	84
Epiphany Last Transfiguration	Matthew 17:1-9	148
Lent 1	Matthew 3:16 – 4:11	12
Lent 2	Matthew 17:1-9	148
Lent 4	1 Samuel 16:11-13	3
Proper 4 [9]	Matthew 7:24-27	84
Proper 5 [10]	Matthew 9:9-13	102
Trinity Sunday	Matthew 28:16-20	222
Proper 6 [11]	Matthew 9:37-38	108
	Matthew 10:1-8, 16	108
Proper 9 [14]	Matthew 11:16-30	116
Proper 10 [15]	Matthew 13:1-9	121
Proper 14 [19]	Matthew 14:22-33	127
Proper 16 [21]	Matthew 16:13-20	142
Proper 18 [23]	Matthew 18:15-20	152
Proper 19 [24]	Matthew 18:21-35	160
	Romans 14:3-11	159
Proper 20 [25]	Matthew 20:1-16	166

Sermon Texts in Lectionary Order

Date	Text	Page

Cycle A (Continued)

Proper 24 [29]	Matthew 22:15-22	178
Proper 25 [30]	Matthew 22:34-40	192
Proper 26 [31]	Matthew 23:1-12	197, 202
	1 Thessalonians 2:9-13	202
All Saints	Matthew 5:1-12	37
Proper 28 [33]	Matthew 25:14-30	209
Reign of Christ [34]	Matthew 25:31-46	218

Cycle B

Thanksgiving	Matthew 6:24-34	54

Cycle C

Baptism of the Lord	Isaiah 43:1-7	93
Proper 8 [13]	Galatians 5:13-25	75

Cycle ABC

New Year	Matthew 25:31-46	218

Additional Scripture Passages Referenced

Text	Title	Page
Genesis		
1:3	All Authority	225
1:11-12	Free to Bear Good Fruit	77
1:26-27	Reckoning	181
1:26-28	Big Shots, Beware!	199
1:27	The Teacher's Take on Taxes	191
3:1-6	Tempted As We Are	20
3:1-6	Big Shots, Beware!	199
37:4-28	Tempted As We Are	20
50:15-21	If Your Brother Sins	155
Exodus		
3:7-15	Walking with Jesus	138
19:1-6	Tempted As We Are	19
Leviticus		
19:2	Bizarre Blessings	44
19:34	The Greatest Commandment	194
26:4	A Lesson in Prayer	52
Deuteronomy		
6:5	The Greatest Commandment	194
7:14	Bizarre Blessings	40
11:11-14	A Lesson in Prayer	52
18:15	Listen to Jesus	151
28:3-6	Bizarre Blessings	40
29:29	A Question of Identity	146
2 Samuel		
5:1-5	Inauguration Day	6
7:12	Inauguration Day	6
7:12	Build Your House	88
7:16	Inauguration Day	6
1 Kings		
18:19-40	Tempted As We Are	19

Additional Scripture Passages Referenced

Text	Title	Page
2 Kings		
25:6-7, 27-30	Inauguration Day	6
Job		
1:21	Required to Risk	215
Psalms		
1:1	Bizarre Blessings	41
2:1-2	Bizarre Blessings	41
18:27	Big Shots, Beware!	200
23:4	Just Ask	73
24:1	Tempted As We Are	21
24:1	It's Not Fair!	175
32:1	Bizarre Blessings	40
33:12	Bizarre Blessings	40
40:4	Bizarre Blessings	40
41:1	Bizarre Blessings	41
84:4	Bizarre Blessings	40
89:15	Bizarre Blessings	41
106:3	Bizarre Blessings	41
112:1	Bizarre Blessings	41
127:1	Build Your House	88
139:13-18	The Greatest Commandment	194
Proverbs		
3:5	Big Shots, Beware!	199
3:6	Tempted As We Are	19
14:21	Bizarre Blessings	41
28:14	Bizarre Blessings	40
29:18	Bizarre Blessings	40
Isaiah		
6:1	All Authority	226
26:3	God's Wellness Plan	35
26:3	A Lesson in Prayer	52
30:18	Bizarre Blessings	40

Additional Scripture Passages Referenced

Text	Title	Page
Isaiah (Continued)		
43:14	Just Passing Through	97
43:15	Bizarre Blessings	44
53:5-6	Inauguration Day	9
56:1-2	Bizarre Blessings	40
Jeremiah		
17:7	Bizarre Blessings	40
Hosea		
11:1-9	Just Passing Through	97
13:4-5	Tempted As We Are	19
Joel		
2:23	A Lesson in Prayer	52
Zechariah		
10:1	A Lesson in Prayer	52
Matthew		
1:1	Inauguration Day	8
1:20-21	Inauguration Day	9
1:25	The New Guy in Town	23
2:1-2, 7-11	The New Guy in Town	23
2:13-14	The New Guy in Town	23
2:16	The New Guy in Town	23
2:19-23	The New Guy in Town	23
3:13-17	The New Guy in Town	23
4:1-11	The New Guy in Town	24
4:4	Will You Give Them Stones?	64
4:8	All Authority	224
4:8-9	The Games of Childhood	118
4:10-11	Tempted As We Are	20
4:12	The New Guy in Town	24
4:24	God's Wellness Plan	32

Additional Scripture Passages Referenced

Text	Title	Page
Matthew (Continued)		
4:24	A Lesson in Leadership	206
5:9	Bizarre Blessings	45
5:44	A Lesson in Prayer	50
5:45	It's Not Fair!	175
7:11	A Lesson in Prayer	51
7:23	A Question of Identity	147
7:28-29	Divine Assignment	109
8:3, 15	God's Wellness Plan	32
8:5-13	God's Wellness Plan	32
8:19	Bizarre Blessings	45
9:11	Bizarre Blessings	45
9:20-21	God's Wellness Plan	32
9:28	God's Wellness Plan	33
10:28	God's Wellness Plan	35
11:4-5	Divine Assignment	110
11:29	Big Shots, Beware!	201
12:14	What a Surprise!	219
12:34	Tempted As We Are	20
12:38	Bizarre Blessings	45
12:43-45	Tempted As We Are	21
13:40-43	Divine Assignment	111
13:44-46	Sowing Seeds—Bearing Fruit	125
13:54-58	God's Wellness Plan	32
14:1-11	The Teacher's Take on Taxes	188
14:22-23	A Lesson in Prayer	49
14:23	A Lesson in Prayer	48
14:35-36	God's Wellness Plan	32
15:38	Look Who's Invited to Dinner	105
16:1-4	Divine Assignment	110
16:24	Listen to Jesus	151
16:26	The Problem with Prosperity	58
18:13	Inauguration Day	7
18:21-22	If Your Brother Sins	154
19:13	A Lesson in Prayer	49
19:16-30	The Problem with Prosperity	59

Additional Scripture Passages Referenced

Text	Title	Page

Matthew (Continued)

20:16	Bizarre Blessings	43
20:32	God's Wellness Plan	33
21:12	The Teacher's Take on Taxes	190
21:22	A Lesson in Prayer	50
21:23-27	Divine Assignment	110
21:28-32	The Teacher's Take on Taxes	187
21:33-41	The Teacher's Take on Taxes	187
21:43	The Teacher's Take on Taxes	187
22:1-7	The Teacher's Take on Taxes	187
22:16, 24, 36	Bizarre Blessings	45
22:21	Rendering	180
22:22	The Teacher's Take on Taxes	187
23:1-3	Inauguration Day	7
23:11	Big Shots, Beware!	200
24:29-31	What a Surprise!	220
24:36	What a Surprise!	221
25:14-29	Rendering	184
25:31-46	Just Passing Through	99
25:34	Bizarre Blessings	44
26:3-4	What a Surprise!	219
26:39	A Lesson in Prayer	48
26:41	A Lesson in Prayer	50
26:42	A Lesson in Prayer	49
26:49	Bizarre Blessings	45
27:46	A Lesson in Prayer	49
28:19-20	A Lesson in Leadership	203
28:20	What a Surprise!	221

Mark

4:35-39	A Lesson in Leadership	206
5:26-36	God's Wellness Plan	33
6:32-44	Divine Assignment	110
7:32-37	A Lesson in Prayer	49
8:23	God's Wellness Plan	32
8:36	Bizarre Blessings	43

Additional Scripture Passages Referenced

Text	Title	Page
Mark (Continued)		
9:17-27	Just Ask	72
10:14	The Games of Childhood	117
10:46-52	God's Wellness Plan	32
13:11	Tempted As We Are	18
14:32-42	A Lesson in Prayer	49
Luke		
1:26-31	Inauguration Day	8,9
2:4-14	The New Guy in Town	23
2:8-11	Inauguration Day	9
2:22	The New Guy in Town	23
2:22-38	Inauguration Day	9
2:42-47	Inauguration Day	9
3:21-22	A Lesson in Prayer	48
4:16-30	The New Guy in Town	24
4:36	Bizarre Blessings	39
4:36	Divine Assignment	109
5:12-16	A Lesson in Prayer	49
5:16	A Lesson in Prayer	48
5:17	Divine Assignment	109
6:12	A Lesson in Prayer	48
6:12-13	A Lesson in Prayer	49
6:20	Bizarre Blessings	41
6:28	A Lesson in Prayer	50
7:11-15	Tempted As We Are	21
7:47	If Your Brother Sins	154
8:26-36	Divine Assignment	110
8:49-55	Tempted As We Are	21
9:1	Tempted As We Are	20
9:18	A Lesson in Prayer	48
9:28-35	A Lesson in Prayer	49
10:17-19	Tempted As We Are	20
10:17-21	A Lesson in Prayer	49
10:25-37	Divine Assignment	110
10:30-35	Sowing Seeds—Bearing Fruit	125

Additional Scripture Passages Referenced

Text	Title	Page
Luke (Continued)		
11:1	A Lesson in Prayer	48
11:9	A Lesson in Prayer	50
12:16-21	The Problem with Prosperity	58
15:4-7	If Your Brother Sins	153
15:11-32	Sowing Seeds—Bearing Fruit	125
18:1	A Lesson in Prayer	50
18:9-14	A Lesson in Prayer	51
18:10-12	Tempted As We Are	20
18:18-30	The Problem with Prosperity	59
18:22	Look Who's Coming to Dinner	106
19:1-10	The Problem with Prosperity	59
19:10	God's Wellness Plan	31
19:41-44	A Lesson in Prayer	49
21:36	A Lesson in Prayer	50
22:17, 19	A Lesson in Prayer	49
22:32	A Lesson in Prayer	49
23:34	A Lesson in Prayer	49
23:34	If Your Brother Sins	155
23:34	All Authority	225
23:46	A Lesson in Prayer	49
24:44	Listen to Jesus	151
John		
1:4	Sowing Seeds—Bearing Fruit	124
1:12	Sowing Seeds—Bearing Fruit	124
1:18	Sowing Seeds—Bearing Fruit	126
3:1-21	Look Who's Invited to Dinner	105
3:14	Tempted As We Are	21
3:16	Inauguration Day	8
3:16	Tempted As We Are	16
4:3-26	Look Who's Invited to Dinner	105
4:42	Inauguration Day	9
5:6	God's Wellness Plan	33
5:19-20	Big Shots, Beware!	201
6:1-13	Look Who's Invited to Dinner	105

Additional Scripture Passages Referenced

| Text | Title | Page |
|---|---|---|//

John (Continued)

6:1-13	A Lesson in Leadership	206
6:11	A Lesson in Prayer	49
8:44	Tempted As We Are	20
9:6	God's Wellness Plan	32
10:10	Inauguration Day	10
10:10	Divine Assignment	110
11:38-44	Free to Bear Good Fruit	79
11:41	A Lesson in Prayer	49
11:43-44	Tempted As We Are	21
12:28	A Lesson in Prayer	49
12:32	Tempted As We Are	21
13:1-14	Big Shots, Beware!	201
13:2-5	A Lesson in Leadership	206
14:1-3	Bizarre Blessings	44
14:2-3	Just Passing Through	100
14:12	God's Wellness Plan	35
14:16-17	Tempted As We Are	17
14:16-17	All Authority	225
14:18	Step Out!	132
15:15	Tempted As We Are	18
16:33	Walking with Jesus	139
17	A Lesson in Prayer	48
17:20-21	A Lesson in Prayer	49
18:28-40	What a Surprise!	219
19:1-16	What a Surprise!	219
19:30	A Lesson in Prayer	49

Acts

2:21	Inauguration Day	10
5:30-31	All Authority	225
9:1-16	Free to Bear Good Fruit	79
16:31	Inauguration Day	10

Romans

1:18-32	Tempted As We Are	14

Additional Scripture Passages Referenced

Text	Title	Page
Romans (continued)		
3:10	Inauguration Day	9
3:23	Inauguration Day	9
3:23	Tempted As We Are	13
3:23	Tempted As We Are	21
5:1-8	Bizarre Blessings	44
5:5	Tempted As We Are	18
5:9-10	Inauguration Day	10
6:23	Tempted As We Are	16
8:2	Free to Bear Good Fruit	79
8:10	God's Wellness Plan	34
8:11	Just Passing Through	100
8:14-17	Bizarre Blessings	45
8:26-27	A Lesson in Prayer	51
8:29	Rendering	181
8:34	All Authority	225
8:38-39	Step Out!	132
8:38-39	All Authority	226
12:2	The New Guy in Town	28
12:6-8	A Lesson in Leadership	205
1 Corinthians		
2:9	Bizarre Blessings	44
2:9	Listen to Jesus	149
10:13	Tempted As We Are	14
13:11	The Games of Childhood	119
15:22	God's Wellness Plan	35
15:49	Rendering	181
2 Corinthians		
1:22	God's Wellness Plan	35
5:11, 18	Bizarre Blessings	45
5:17-19	Inauguration Day	10
5:20	Bizarre Blessings	45
5:21	Inauguration Day	8

Additional Scripture Passages Referenced

Text	Title	Page

2 Corinthians (Continued)
7:1	Bizarre Blessings	44
8:1-4	Rendering	184
11:14	Tempted As We Are	20

Ephesians
1:7	God's Wellness Plan	35
1:22	Step Out!	131
2:1-5	Bizarre Blessings	44
2:4-7	The Greatest Commandment	194
2:8	Free to Bear Good Fruit	80
2:8-9	Bizarre Blessings	44
2:8-9	If Your Brother Sins	155
3:14-19	The Teacher's Take on Taxes	191
3:20	The Problem with Prosperity	60
4:11-13	Bizarre Blessings	45
4:11-13	A Lesson in Leadership	205
5:2	The Greatest Commandment	194

Philippians
2:5	God's Wellness Plan	34
2:9-11	A Question of Identity	147
2:10-11	Inauguration Day	7
3:10	Bizarre Blessings	44
4:7	If Your Brother Sins	156
4:11	The Problem with Prosperity	60
4:19	The Teacher's Take on Taxes	191

Colossians
1:15-16	Inauguration Day	6
1:15	Rendering	181
1:19	Sowing Seeds—Bearing Fruit	126
1:19	A Question of Identity	146
1:20	All Authority	225
2:9	A Question of Identity	146

Additional Scripture Passages Referenced

Text	Title	Page
1 Thessalonians		
4:16-17	Just Passing Through	100
5:17	A Lesson in Prayer	53
1 Timothy		
6:10	The Problem with Prosperity	58
6:15	Inauguration Day	6
2 Timothy		
2:4, 15	Tempted As We Are	19
4:1	All Authority	225
Titus		
3:3-7	A Lesson in Leadership	206
Hebrews		
2:14-15	Inauguration Day	9
2:14	Tempted As We Are	16
4:15	Inauguration Day	8
4:15	Tempted As We Are	13
6:4-5	If Your Brother Sins	156
7:24-25	Step Out!	134
7:27	What a Surprise!	220
9:27	God's Wellness Plan	35
11:16	Bizarre Blessings	44
James		
1:14-15	Tempted As We Are	16
2:10	Free to Bear Good Fruit	80
4:2-3	Just Ask	74
4:7	Tempted As We Are	20
1 Peter		
5:7	Listen to Jesus	150

Additional Scripture Passages Referenced

Text	Title	Page
1 John		
1:9	Tempted As We Are	17
2:1	Step Out!	134
2:1-2	Tempted As We Are	16
3:1	Bizarre Blessings	45
3:2	Bizarre Blessings	44
4:1	Tempted As We Are	20
4:1, 6	Listen to Jesus	151
4:4	Tempted As We Are	18
4:13	Tempted As We Are	18
4:14	Inauguration Day	9
4:19	The Greatest Commandment	194
Revelation		
3:20	Inauguration Day	9
7:9-17	All Authority	225
11:15	Inauguration Day	6
17:14	Inauguration Day	6
19:16	Inauguration Day	6
22:5	Inauguration Day	6

www.ingramcontent.com/pod-product-compliance
Lightning Source LLC
Chambersburg PA
CBHW020849090426
42736CB00008B/300